Searching for Gomez

GWENDA GRAY

ISBN: 978-1-7636896-0-2 (Paperback)

ISBN: 978-1-7636896-1-9 (eBook)

Published by Gwenda Gray

Golden Beach 4551

Sunshine Coast, Australia.

Contents

Gomez the Puppy

Gomez and Monty

A real athlete

Gomez going through his Cancer Treatment

Gomez and Priya

His favourite position

. . .

Gomez and Charlotte

Gomez's 15th Birthday on 1st August 2022

Gomee and Charlotte

Gomee the Senior Boy

Prologue

Maybe unconditional love reaches a whole new level when it is shown in mature and quiet ways.

I knew how lucky I was to have been loved in that way. To be seen as perfect, loveable and good! To experience the type of love that keeps our hearts open and helps us embrace our kindness and patience. The type of love that gives us so much joy, laughter and tears. The type of love that can fill or break our heart.

His dependency on me during the last year meant that I needed to be there for him. How would he survive without me? He needed me to care for him, give him his medicine and soothe his fears. We kept close together, where he felt safe and secure. If he could not find me, he became anxious, breathing raggedly and rapidly, and this only eased once he was close to me again.

I still did all the things that made him feel happy and alive, and I loved seeing him that way. His old face reflected his younger self, full of energy, mischief and a zest for life. I loved him so much.

I knew that he probably did not have much longer to live. I looked into his eyes each day and asked him if he was okay. When his eyes smiled back into mine, I had my answer. I had thought it through and knew how I would support him when the time came. I had a plan, as I had for those who came before him. It broke my heart to think about it, but it was what I had to do. I would try to make sure that he died peacefully, without pain and knowing that he was loved. I would be with him, holding him, so that he felt safe and loved to his last breath.

But, as is often the case, the universe had other plans. He apparently had one more adventure to experience before that time came. A harmless impulsive adventure which went wrong very quickly. An adventure where he forgot his age and vulnerability for a moment, and by the time he remembered, it was too late and too difficult to turn back.

An adventure which would touch the hearts of so many in the community, who responded to my pleas for help. A community who saw a need and responded with pure and open hearts. A community who fell in love with him and wanted him to be safe. A community who worked tirelessly for six days to bring him safely back where he belonged. To bring him back to me.

I am your Dog

AUTHOR UNKNOWN

I am the one who always waits for you.
Your car has a special sound that I have imprinted on my senses and I can recognize it among a thousand.
Your steps have a magic timbre.
Your voice is music to my ears.
If I see your joy, it makes me happy!
Your scent is the best.
Your presence is what moves my senses.
Your awakening wakes me up.
I watch you sleep and for me you are my everything.
Your gaze is a ray of light.
Your hands on me have the lightness of peace and the sublime display of infinite love.
When you go out, I feel a huge emptiness in my heart.
I wait for you again and again.
I am the one who will wait for you all my life
Today, tomorrow and always:
I am your dog.

Day One

MONDAY 10TH OCTOBER 2022

The morning was rainy and cool, but as usual, I drove my two Golden Retrievers, Gomez and Priya, to the dog park in Buderim. The rain had put people off, so there were only two people there with their dogs. I knew both from other visits to the dog park.

As the dogs ran around in the rain, we joked about being crazy dog owners who braved the weather, unlike so many who had not turned up at the usual time.

Gomez slowly chased his ball a few times. I threw it a short distance, knowing his limitations, but he still loved to chase the ball, even at his advanced age of fifteen years. Any sign of difficulty was only shown on the way back to me, when he limped a little, and was slow in his gait. Gomez had quite severe arthritis, but his passion for the ball, and his medications, meant that he could still enjoy his favourite activity. If he had the energy, he would bring the ball back to me, so that I could throw it again. If not, Gomez would find something far more important to do, such as chew a stick. This is how he paced himself. The ball was always close to him. Once Gomez was rested, he would bring the ball back to me for another chase.

Priya, at seven years of age, had far more energy, but no real commitment to the ball. I was always searching for her ball, and that morning Dave, who always helped me to find the ball when it was missing, was at the dog park. It was a standing joke between us, with me confessing to having a type of "dog ball blindness".

We did not stay for long that morning, as the rain became heavier and we were all getting quite wet as we huddled under a very small pergola. I headed home with Gomez and Priya, and after their breakfast, I dried the dogs, put the heater on, and a blanket over Gomee. As a senior dog, he had lost most of his muscle and any fat, and was quite thin, so he felt the cold.

I then went out to the gym, and on my way home did some grocery shopping. When I arrived home in the early afternoon, my son came downstairs to help me carry the shopping bags upstairs to the shared kitchen. I had parked outside the garage, and thought that I had closed the garage door with the fob. Before going upstairs to unpack the shopping with my son, I quickly checked the dogs and opened the downstairs door so that they could go out to the fenced back garden.

We had been living at this rental property in Buderim for two months, having moved to the Sunshine Coast to purchase a dual occupancy house. My son had just spent a few days in Melbourne, packing up my old house there. He was exhausted after driving back in a small truck, arriving back in Buderim the night before. We talked about how our lives were going as I unpacked the shopping, and this developed into quite an in-depth and emotional discussion about the stresses of moving, finances, real estate agents, his unhappiness with his work and having to work nights in Brisbane through the coming week. The last year had been challenging in every way. We had left our homes and friends in Melbourne, and were trying to sell our homes there without much success. We had to sell in order to buy on the Sunshine Coast, and money was already getting tight. My son was working from home in a new role, my daughter in law had just secured work and it had taken time to find a kindergarten spot for my granddaughter. As we talked, my son and I agreed that we had too much to deal with and could not cope with any more problems.

At one point during our discussion, I heard some barking downstairs from the dogs. We were in the middle of talking, and I ignored the barking, thinking that Gomez and Priya were just having their regular noisy rumble. The noise from the dogs stopped after a couple of minutes.

I went back downstairs at about 3pm, and immediately noticed the sunlight coming through the garage. I saw that the garage door was open. My stomach turned over, and I quickly checked that the dogs were there. Priya was there, but there was no sign of Gomez. I thought that he must be outside in the garden, so I searched for him there. Being deaf, I knew he could not hear me, so I clapped my hands and used a high pitched voice which usually drew his attention. He was not inside or outside. Where was he? Why was Priya there, but Gomez was not? I could feel my heart thumping, and tears came to my eyes.

Gomez had always been interested in what was beyond the garage door. Despite being old, he was an inquisitive dog, and always ready for an adventure. Gomez had recently noticed the brush turkeys outside the garden fence and had joined Priya in barking at them. I went outside the garage, and noticed that there was fresh dog poo there, in a trail up the drive. He had gone up the steep drive. What would have enticed him up the drive? Perhaps he had chased a brush turkey, but, if so, why had Priya stayed at home? Or had she gone with him then come home again? I started to feel extremely panicky and short of breath. I felt faint, and my body felt weak, like I was going to fall over. My thoughts were racing, but at some level I felt sure that he could not have gone far due to his age and limited mobility. He had already been out to the dog park in the morning, and that usually took all his energy. I tried to reassure myself: Gomez must have just gone for a short wander, maybe across the road, or just down the road a little.

But Gomez was nowhere to be seen. I rushed back to the house, screamed out to my son that Gomez was missing, put Priya on the lead and the three of us took off on foot looking for him. As we rushed up the driveway, my thoughts seemed to be out of control. He could get run over, as he could not hear cars and had no road sense. People were starting to come home from work, and some people drove too fast along this road. I told Priya to find Gomez, asking her 'where's Gomez? where's Gomez?' over and over. Just at the top of the drive, to the right, she whimpered, but we could not see or hear Gomez. I decided that, as an anxious dog, she was reacting to my high level of anxiety, and had no idea where he was. My mind was racing by this time, and I was experiencing intense feelings of anxiety, fear, panic and horror.

My son decided to use the car to search for Gomez down the road and side roads, and I searched on foot in the other direction with Priya. There were a few people on the road, walking their dogs, and a neighbour I had met a few times, Jenny, came out of her house to see what was happening. I told everyone who I came across that Gomez was missing. Nobody had seen Gomez, but everyone said that they would look out for him. Then my son came back, having found no sign of Gomez, and I went out in the car to look. I had no idea where to look, I was shaking and in no fit state to drive. I returned home quickly. We realised that it was nearly 5pm, so my son needed to go to pick up his wife and daughter from kindergarten in Kuluin. We only had the one car, so he had to leave.

I had no idea what to do, but I knew that I had to put everything I had into finding my precious boy, Gomez. He needed me, and I had to find him quickly. Night was approaching fast, and we would run out of light. I realised that I could not physically search due to my mobility issues, but I could use social media to try to reach people who could help. I rushed back into the house and decided to put a post on the local Facebook community page, asking for help to find Gomez. I had used a Facebook community page a few years before in Melbourne, when I needed volunteers to help walk the dogs after I had multiple surgeries and could not do it myself. At that time, I had a large number of people offering to help, so I thought it was worth trying to reach out to people in that way again. I hoped that some people might respond to my post, or at least spread the word so that somebody might see Gomez somewhere.

I was new to the Sunshine Coast, so did not know about the many lost dog pages on Facebook. It would have been useful to post on those pages immediately, but luckily people who saw my post on the community page shared to those lost dog pages.

> **My post on the Facebook community page was worded:**
>
> *My white Golden Retriever is missing from Jarrah Road Buderim. He is 15 and deaf, and his name is Gomez. He will be disoriented and scared and I am SO worried about him.*

I chose a recent photo, which was a headshot and showed his age, vulnerability and beautiful face.

I heard somebody moaning with pain and realised that it was me. There was heaviness in my chest, and pressure which felt like a loud wail pushing to burst out. It had hit me. My baby boy was missing, and I had no way of keeping him safe. He needed me, and I had failed him. My thoughts were racing, and I felt guilty and responsible. Why hadn't I checked that the garage door was closed? Because we were in a rental, I was not familiar with the "fob", but I should have checked. Had I bumped it in my pocket? Had it malfunctioned? Why hadn't I checked what the barking was? How could he have disappeared in such a short time? My job was to look after my precious senior boy, and to keep him safe. I had failed!

I had to find him.

My daughter-in-law and granddaughter returned, and they started to search down some of the nearby steep drives. The light was beginning to fade, as sunset was just before 6pm, and it was also time for my son to take the car to go to work in Brisbane. My daughter-in-law made a "lost dog" poster, and my son said he would put them up around the area when he returned in the early morning.

I started searching again with my torch, but the battery went flat. I was going door to door, and someone at one of the houses kindly lent me another torch, but that did not take long to go flat as well. I asked everyone out on the street if they had seen my old Golden Retriever, and some people were confused, as I had Priya, a Golden Retriever, on the lead. I doubt that I was making much sense, and my brain was slow to register that some of the people I asked probably thought that I was a highly confused older woman who had imagined that I had lost my dog. I was unable to go down steep drives because of my mobility problems, and I started to realise that I was unable to search for him myself due to my physical limitations. I felt useless, and knew that I urgently needed as much help as I could get.

About an hour after I posted on Facebook that Gomez was missing, a few people arrived and asked if they could help, including Evan and Brigitte, who said that they had seen the post. My neighbour, Jenny, was already searching places as well. She, and a young man, Jamie, took their utes into the bush close to the house, and used the strong lights to look for any sign of Gomez. They could not drive far into the bush as it was so steep and inaccessible. Other people were in another part of the bush with torches. Surely one of these people would find Gomez. My precious boy could not have gone far.

A couple of hours passed, and nobody found any sign of him. I knew I needed to get some sleep and rest so that I was at my best to search for Gomez the next day, but real sleep never came. I tossed and turned, thoughts and fears racing, and tears surfacing. I had never had a dog go missing, and I had no idea how that would feel. It was like my heart had been ripped out of me. He needed me, and the thought of him somewhere alone and possibly injured, was unbearable.

Each time I dropped off to sleep I jolted awake and remembered that he was missing. I kept straining to hear any sound that could have been Gomez. I checked Facebook every few minutes, thinking that somebody might post that they had either seen Gomez, or had taken him into their care. A large number of people had already commented on my post, expressing sympathy for my situation, and many others had shared my post to other Facebook sites, including the numerous "lost dog" sites on the Sunshine Coast.

My head throbbed, my heart raced, tears sat in my throat and eyes and I felt absolutely overwhelmed. But I also knew that, if I was to find Gomez, I had to be strong and manage these unbearable feelings. Somehow I was going to find him.

Gomez My Heart Dog

One of the greatest gifts we receive from dogs is the tenderness they evoke in us. ~ Dean Koontz

I have always had a strong need for love and understanding, after growing up in a family environment where love and understanding were conditional and sporadic. While I appear confident and capable, my independence originated through necessity. I needed to care for myself from an early age in my family of origin, then at boarding school for six years, and then as a single person for most of my life. While appearing strong, I am a very sensitive person who is easily hurt. I can overthink and turn things over in my mind far too much. For much of my life I have taken things personally, and I have needed to learn that often another person's behaviour has nothing to do with me. I have worked hard to accept myself and have come to really like many of my qualities, such as kindness, warmth, intelligence and persistence. I am very fortunate that I have some wonderful family members and friends who love me.

Throughout my life, however, my dogs have given me the unconditional love and acceptance that I deeply needed. This has been offered without judgement, and I have received it without fear of rejection. I have always known that they loved me, and I have not had to second guess what they meant or how they felt, because I just knew. I could trust their love without the doubts and insecurities that so often crept into my relationships with people. My dogs have all given me unconditional love, and it has been returned with my gratitude, love and recognition of their vulnerability. As a child I was fortunate to be given this love by our family dog, Baron. I could tell him my secrets and worries, and he would listen attentively, looking at me adoringly. I have loved all my dogs so very much, and have always been an attentive, caring and protective dog mum. My dogs have been incredibly important to me.

Many people who have dogs do not have the close relationship of a true dog lover. They love their dog, but the dog is not a member of the family. They do not give the dog the affection and love they deserve. Many families are too busy with day-to-day life and the dog can become a bit of a nuisance to them. I see myself as a true "dog person" who has really loved each of my dogs. Their welfare has been very important to me, and I see it as my responsibility to ensure that all their needs are met in order for them to be happy and healthy. That is my choice, for many reasons, but it fills my heart to be loved by a dog. It has also broken my heart more than a few times through my life.

The term "heart dog" has developed to describe those dogs with whom we have a special and deep connection. Those dogs who can be described as a "soulmate". I believe that I have been lucky enough to have had two heart dogs in my life, where my bond with them was exceptionally strong. My first dog as an adult was Sam, a rescue dog who formed an immediate bond with me, trusting me from the very first day. He knew that I would never hurt him and that he was safe with me. With Sam, I experienced a strong loving bond which felt very special, and I have such gratitude to Sam for the years he gave me. The loyalty he showed to me, and then to my son as a baby and young child, was amazing for a dog who had been beaten and neglected in his early life.

As a single person for much of my life, my dogs have offered steady companionship and have filled a space in my heart. The loss of each of my dogs has been a deep and painful experience, and I hold them all dear in my heart. But the intense pain which comes with losing a heart dog shocked me when I lost Sam over forty years ago, and then again when Gomez went missing.

Gomez was my Gomee, Baby Boy, Beautiful Boy, Precious and Mezzy. I probably realised that he was my heart dog when there was a risk of losing him to cancer at four years of age. Until then, Gomez had tested my patience as an overly energetic and naughty pup, and we were only just beginning to settle into an easier relationship. I had always loved him, and I knew that there was something special about him. When he had the diagnosis of a malignant tumour, I did not question the need to do everything I possibly could to help him to fight the cancer. I knew that he had the strength to do so, but that he also needed my help and unswerving commitment. I felt the intensity of our attachment and recognised that Gomez was my second heart dog. That bond kept us both motivated through a challenging year of surgeries and chemotherapy, heartbreak when the tumour returned and then joy with his unexpected recovery.

For most of the years spent with Gomez I lived on my own. I believe that being a single person intensified the relationships I had with my dogs, and is a different dynamic to a family dog. Losing a dog as an older, single person, seems to be far more challenging because of that bond.

I still felt young and fit when Gomez came to live with me, and his life span marked a big change for me. I went from somebody in my early fifties to a much older person in my very late sixties. Through those years, my body underwent huge changes as arthritis took its toll and necessitated three surgeries. My confidence was affected by these changes in mobility and also by an accident in the dog park where my ankle was shattered. I also retired during Gomez's life span, which once again sparked a crisis of confidence and identity. Gomez gave me the support I needed to get through those challenges. Somebody once said to me that our dogs replace what is missing in our hearts. I know that I missed being a full time mother, I missed being in a loving relationship with a partner, I missed having a strong functioning body and I missed my professional identity. As my life and perception of myself changed, my dogs were a constant for me, loving me without judgement.

I retired from work a few weeks before Covid was announced as a serious illness. Gomez and Priya helped me to get through the dark times of the Melbourne Covid lockdowns, not just at home, but by going to the nearby dog park each day and having socially distanced and masked chats with a few wonderful people there. I depended on the dogs to keep me company and to keep me motivated. I needed them as much as they needed me. I have always talked to my dogs, and at times, answered for them.

> *No one appreciates the very special genius of your conversation as the dog does.*
> *~ Christopher Morley*

Some dogs are trained to be "emotional support dogs", and others are naturally so, without any specific training. Gomez was a "natural", taking on this role with a cheerful and wonderfully distracting style. He did not like it if I was upset, but would just get close to me, and often do something quite silly, where I had no choice but to laugh. Gomez did a wonderful job of looking after me, through health scares, heartbreak, bereavements, moving from Sydney to Melbourne, surgeries and hospitalisations. He adjusted well to different people looking after him (and Priya), when I was in hospital and, afterwards, going through physical rehabilitation. When I asked on a Facebook community page for help to walk two Golden Retrievers, I had a big response, and Gomez won the hearts of those people. Even when I was able to walk the dogs again and take them to the dog park, many of those people would get in touch asking if they could visit and take the dogs out. Gomez had great appeal, and people loved him, and incidentally, those people got to know me and became my friends as well. Nearly all my new friends in Melbourne were made through the dogs, thanks to Gomez's brazen (and correct) belief that everyone loved him.

Gomez did the most wonderful job of looking after me, and I did a wonderful job of looking after him, firstly when he had cancer, and then as he aged and needed special care and attention. He needed me, and I did everything I could to help him to be happy, comfortable and safe. We had a very special relationship, where he always made me feel loved and cared about, and pretty well perfect. My great love for him confirmed what he already knew; That he was perfect and loveable. I also had so much joy from my interactions with him and so many belly laughs. Gomez was such a quirky, funny, affectionate and unique dog.

What a gift!

Gomez, my heart dog.

This was the very special dog who went missing.

Gomez My Senior Boy

Once you have had a wonderful dog, a life without one, is a life diminished. When you have dogs, you witness their uncomplaining acceptance of suffering, their bright desire to make the most of life in spite of the limitations of age and disease, their calm awareness of the approaching end when their final hours come. ~ Dean Koontz

When Gomez went missing, he was a couple of months over fifteen years of age, which is a few years past the average eleven year life expectancy of a Golden Retriever. I had been very lucky that my previous senior boy, Monty, had lived to just under sixteen years of age. As an old dog, Monty had all the expected signs of aging, but was still a happy and loving dog. I had a plan for Monty, and his wonderful vet, Peter, was happy to come to our home when needed at the end of Monty's life, so that Monty slowly left this world being lovingly held by me. I had the same plan for Gomez, when it was his time.

Gomez was given up to three months to live when he was nearly five years of age, after a year's treatment for his malignant cancer. But for some reason, despite his tumour returning, he surpassed all expectations and was always a healthy, happy and energetic dog. Like all senior dogs, he started to develop a few medical issues in his later years. He had another cancer scare necessitating removal of a toe when he was eleven years of age. He lost a lot of weight when he was thirteen, with no obvious cause. As his basic blood tests were good for his age, it was likely he had cancer again. He still appeared healthy and happy, but he had become a frail dog with that weight loss. When Gomez was thirteen, his eyelashes turned inwards and irritated his eyes, and the surgery he had was not really successful. As a result, he had stains coming down from his eyes, like teardrops, despite my constant efforts to clean them.

Gomez's tumour which had grown back years before, became a little larger as he aged, and the resulting pressure on his bowel caused incontinence. He needed constant care and reassurance, and I spent time gently cleaning him up after his accidents. Gomez had also gradually developed arthritis over a few years, and this was managed by a range of medications and regular gentle exercise. He was also very deaf, and only responded to a high voice and clapping, unless he could see me, when he responded to eye contact and hand signals. It was rare for me to have a full night's sleep, as I would listen out for him, as he sometimes had what sounded like a panic attack, where his breathing was erratic and ragged until he relaxed to my touch. Of course, as with all senior dogs, I asked the vet regularly if Gomez was still okay. My answers to the questions always asked about senior dogs were that he still loved his food, he still loved going out and would chase the ball a little, he still loved to play with Priya, he still made eye contact and he seemed comfortable. It was not yet time.

After a lifetime of loving us unconditionally, anticipating our needs and working so hard to please us, once our dogs are older it then becomes our turn to protect, care for and love them even more than when they were younger. They need us to be their eyes, their ears, their legs, their advocate and their protector. They need us to patiently and lovingly clean up after them, walk more slowly, give them their medicine and make sure they feel safe. Our strong emotional connection with them means that it is impossible to imagine not worrying about them. When I hear about some older dogs being given up for various reasons, my heart breaks. Or when I hear about dog owners not being able to cope with being with their dogs at the very end, once again, my heart breaks. Our old dogs need us, and it is our duty to ask the questions and listen to the answers in order to determine if they still have quality of life, or whether it is time to make a difficult decision. They need us to have an end of life plan.

When a dog is old, it is a time to put their needs ahead of our own, and they are totally dependent on us to do that for them. After all, they have always put us first. Dogs do not live for very long. But every day is lived to the full, teaching us so many life lessons. Thinking about Gomee's life, he had some big challenges, but mainly he lived a life of joy, love and silliness. He always knew that he was loved, and he was so loving. He was funny and cheeky, a terrible show-off and so confident!

As an old boy Gomez still had the naughtiness and humour of a pup, but his body was no longer one. He was skinny, he limped, and, as mentioned, he had ongoing problems with his eyes, lost most of his hearing and started losing control of his bowels. While he still lived life to the full, he knew he needed some extra help and accepted it from me.

This was the beautiful and vulnerable senior dog who went missing.

Gomez needed me, his medicine and the safety of home.

He did not need to be on his own in the hostile bush.

The Bush

Early in 2022, my son, his family and I made the big decision to move to the Sunshine Coast. We had been living in Melbourne for a few years, which included the Covid lockdowns, and like many others, decided that we wanted a change in lifestyle. My son had researched a few different areas where we could move to and find a dual living home, and we decided on the Sunshine Coast, as we had family there and I had spent wonderful times there about fifty years ago.

We had a lot of difficulty finding a rental property to live in while looking to purchase the right home for us all. Many people had made similar decisions to us, mainly due to Covid, and rentals were hard to find coming from outside of the local area. Local people were finding it increasingly difficult to find affordable rentals, and there was some ill feeling towards people moving to the area from outside the state.

My son and I were both trying to sell property in Melbourne, and were not having much success, as the bottom had fallen out of the property market there. Meantime the prices of homes on the Sunshine Coast were rising. While still living in Melbourne, finding a rental property on the Sunshine Coast seemed close to impossible, even though my niece was able to inspect some for us. It became very stressful, as we could not move up to the Sunshine Coast until we found something. I had two dogs, so this added to the difficulty. Even though tenants are now able to have dogs, it no doubt played a part in our lack of success.

We finally found a property to rent. The owners planned to return to live at the property after four and a half months, so it was no doubt difficult for them to find tenants to sign such a short lease. It was large and we thought it would suit us, despite the high price. My dogs were accepted by the owners. The description of the property said that it had ten acres of bush, but that the back garden was fenced.

At the end of July 2022, I drove the dogs 1,859 kilometres from Melbourne to the rented house in North Buderim. I knew that it had to be me who drove that distance with them, as any alternative would be too stressful, particularly for Gomez. He needed me with him. The first night we stayed in the ACT, then 2 nights and a day on the north coast of NSW. It was an exhausting drive for me, coupled with the worry of how an old dog, at nearly 15, would cope. On the first day, at one rest stop, he was so stiff he could barely walk, and I feared he would not survive the trip. But apart from being extremely tired, he managed very well.

It was not until we moved into the rental property that we saw what the ten acres of bush was like. The thick canopy of enormous eucalypts and turpentines shaded a treacherous area of hostile and unwelcoming bush. It had not been maintained for many years, and the thick and overgrown lantana hid the steep and sudden drops, large holes and tangled vines. The area dropped away steeply from the house to an industrial area about 500 metres below. Even an avid bush lover would not feel welcome in this bush. The road was on the crest of a hill, with all driveways dropping away steeply.

From the house and back garden it was impossible to see any distance. I had grown up next to a forest in Sydney and had also lived in the bush for some years as an adult, but this was something totally different. I remember my father removing any sign of lantana in the bush where I grew up. This bushland was absolutely full of it. It was also home to many dangerous creatures: snakes, spiders, ticks and leeches, to name a few.

This is the bush where Gomez was lost. We had only been at the property for a short time, and, as a city dog, he was totally unfamiliar with that or any other bush.

This is the bush where wonderful people bravely searched for Gomez.

Old Dogs Wander Off to Die

When Gomez went missing, many people suggested to me that at fifteen years of age, he had probably wandered off to die alone.

Some older animals do that, particularly cats, but not my Gomez.

I will explain why.

Gomee never did anything quietly. He liked centre stage, was confident and a dreadful show off! He was funny, cheeky, active and full of bravado.

He never thought he misbehaved, but he was the naughtiest puppy I have ever known!

Gomez fought a dreadful cancer at 4 years of age. He had surgeries and a year of chemotherapy, but when the tumour returned, he was given up to 3 months to live. He had no intention of meeting those expectations. He had a lot more living to do and refused to die as predicted! The experts could never work out why he survived.

Even as an old dog, he had the respect of younger dogs at the dog park. If he asked them to move away, they did, even though they could have easily knocked him down if they had tried.

Gomez had a powerful aura.

Gomez also had the ability to find people who needed a lift, and he could somehow ease their pain. Although busy with his ball in the dog park, he would sometimes stop and position himself next to somebody sitting quietly on a seat. Without fail, that person would later say to me that it felt like he knew that they were having a hard day and needed him to cheer them up.

Everyone who met Gomez really loved him. He was well known and loved at the dog parks we frequented in both Sydney and Melbourne. Even though we had only been in Buderim for a couple of months, most people in the dog park there knew his name. He was very good looking in his prime, and people often took photos of him. Being a cream retriever made him unusual for some, and they would want to talk to me about his colour and appearance. He looked people in the eye, and his approach was always friendly and confident. I remember his veterinary nurse confiding in me that Gomez was her favourite dog. His vet in Sydney described his smiling face as like a "cracked watermelon", which was a wonderful image of his huge smile.

Simone, who groomed Gomez a few weeks before he went missing, fell in love with him.

> **In her words:** *I was fortunate to meet Gomez once. I sat on the floor with him after his groom, brushing him, and fell in love. I felt very privileged to spend that time with him there, and felt privileged being trusted with such a special boy. Knowing his incredible story, and also his eyes, something about them ...There was just something about him, something very very special, difficult to explain.....*

My dear friend Laz, who knew him very well, posted these words on Facebook when Gomez went missing:

> **GOMEZ THE WONDER DOG.**
> Gomez was put on this Earth for one purpose.
> To show us what love, courage, faith, understanding and hope are all about.
> He has a love and a zest for life that he has passed on to us.
> He helps those of us who are sick at heart or broken.
> He helps fix us.
> I know he has changed my life.
> Now Gomez needs our help.
> Please everyone who is able, please help him.
> Please help him find his way back home.
> Please God bring Gomez back home to Gwen and her family.

Gomez was tough and confident, but he also had the gentlest soul. He was such a sweetheart.

Despite his bravado, Gomee was a mummy's boy. I found it so difficult when people suggested to me that he had gone off to die on his own. I could not believe that he would have wanted to go somewhere and die alone. My touch and presence helped him to feel safe again. He needed and wanted to be with me.

Gomez somehow inspired a massive group of people to help him and search for him. And those people all fell in love with him as well, despite never meeting him.

Gomez was an extraordinary dog, who lived an extraordinary life, loved with an enormous heart, was loved by all who knew him and so many who never even met him.

He did not wander off to die.

Day Two

TUESDAY 11TH OCTOBER 2022

It was light just after 5am, and I got out of bed, feeling drained, sad and anxious. The first thing I did was to search the house and garden again. I had a flash of inspiration: 'He must be behind the bushes in the front garden!', even though I had already searched all those areas the previous day. I could feel that compulsion rising up in me to search everything again and again, just like when I lost a key or something small. Many of the places I looked did not even make any sense.

My four year old granddaughter came downstairs early, asking if Gomez had come back. She absolutely adored him and was very worried and confused. I tried to be calm and positive for her, and she seemed reassured that we would find him that day.

I had updated my post on Facebook in the early morning, specifically asking for volunteers to help search. Many people had shared my post, and Facebook was already flooded with the story of Gomez, the old and deaf Golden Retriever, who had gone missing. I was stunned by the response. I also paid for a Facebook advertisement on Lost Pet Finders.

I had messages from a large number of people, asking if they could help, and I gratefully accepted all help that was offered. I also followed up all suggestions made. I had never had a dog go missing, so I had no experience in developing a plan of action. Looking back, the search could have been more organised, but it was a heartfelt community response, rather than a well thought out plan. I think that would generally be the case for anybody who lost their dog for the first time.

My thinking was that the more people searching, the more chance of somebody seeing Gomez. He may have been in one spot, or he may have been moving. He may have been in the bush, or huddled in somebody's shed. As I had no idea where he had gone, or what had happened to him, it seemed right to try everything. The only definite facts were that he was an adventurous and inquisitive dog, he had got out through the open garage door, and he had left a poo trail up the drive. I discovered that he had also left some poo down a side path which went to a locked door, and I could not work out why he would have gone there. I shared the information I knew with everybody I met, and they then passed on that information.

It was, however, anyone's guess what had happened to Gomez. At some stage we asked neighbours to check their CCTV cameras, and he had not been seen on any of these. Nobody had seen him. It seemed important to be open to suggestions and to encourage people to follow their 'hunches'. The stress of Gomez going missing was already affecting my thinking, and from memory, I did not stop to consider all possibilities, or go through the facts that I knew. While I may have seemed calm and clear thinking, I am sure that I was not. In retrospect, my emotions, and the emotions of the community, made it difficult to work out the answer to the question of where Gomez was. I suspect that it is always that way when a dog goes missing. Our cognitive abilities are clouded by shock, grief and anxiety.

People started to knock on the door from about 7.30am, and they all genuinely wanted to help. They had seen the Facebook post, and many had shared it to the Sunshine Coast lost dog sites on Facebook. Two women, Sharene and Julie, arrived quite early, and wanted to help by getting flyers printed from the poster. They suggested doorknocking with flyers, and leaving them in letter-boxes if people were not at home. They organised the printing, and told volunteers which areas to cover with the flyers. Sharene looked at a map of the area and divided flyers into different streets in a 2 kilometre radius. I had a message from Dave, saying that he was on his way with a thermal drone, and Jamie was already there, using an ordinary drone. The number of people contacting me or just turning up at the house surprised me. Even though I had posted on Facebook, I had not expected such a large response.

Not everyone wanted to go into the hostile bushland, and I believed that it seemed a bit unlikely that he had gone there, due to his mobility problems. He was a city dog, not used to bush-land, so would not have chosen to go there. His only experience in the bush was the thin coastal bushland next to beaches we had visited in the past. When younger, he had been known to follow the scent of a wallaby or small animal into that type of bush, but he had always come back out quickly. Most people agreed that if Gomez was in the bushland, he would be close by, and he may have fallen and not been able to get back up. The majority thinking was that he would therefore be close to the road or to one of the many steep driveways to houses. Perhaps he had become confused, thinking that another steep drive was our driveway. A few people searched further into the bush, wondering if he may have somehow chased a brush turkey or become disori-ented. It made sense that if Gomez had had a misadventure which ended up in the bush, he would be unable to come back up, due to the steepness, so, if he was able to move, the only way was down.

Kate and Donna, who had Golden Retrievers themselves, searched deep in the bush, and were determined that they would find him. They brought their friend Kellie to help on two days. While there was a high level of concern about him from everybody, there was also a strong sense of hope. All the people there were sure that he would be found quickly. At his age, Gomez could not be far away, unless somebody had picked him up and taken him somewhere.

The drones were not successful in locating him, as the tree canopy was too tall and dense. But efforts with drones continued, just in case he moved to a clearing in the bushland or could be seen on the road somewhere. The thermal drone identified a small body of water some distance down the steep hill, and so Dave and some others searched that area, thinking that if Gomez was in the bush, he would have been thirsty and therefore attracted to water. Lost dogs often look for a water source. By the middle of the day, there were a lot of people in the bush. I had met some of them, or spoken to them on the phone, but I became aware that there were people searching in the bushland who I had not met. They had quietly joined the search and most had met up with other people in the bush. Some messages or calls I had that day asked what they could do to help, and how they could attract Gomez if they did see him. Because of his deafness, I told people that he only responded to clapping or a high "child" voice. His sense of smell was strong, so carrying high value treats would be useful.

As the day progressed, it became clear how hazardous the bush was. Some people were emerging from the bush with scratches and leeches on them, and there was mention of snakes close to some of the searchers. Luckily it was a cloudy and fairly mild day, with a top temperature of about 20 degrees, so if Gomez was in the bush, he would not be getting overheated. Those who went deep into the bush were in agreement that he could not have travelled far due to the terrain. They would get to a steep drop or an inaccessible spot and decided that he would not have gone further.

Many of the people who came to help offered to search the streets, asking people to check sheds or under their houses, put up posters and drop off flyers. An enormous area was covered and I had calls from all over the Sunshine Coast, asking if I had found Gomez. Several businesses in the Kunda Industrial Estate phoned me, saying that they had received flyers, and asking if he had been found.

During the day, I telephoned all the veterinary clinics within about 10 kilometres, and sent posters to any who were on Facebook messenger, so that they had photos of him. Volunteers dropped off posters to other clinics. I also phoned the council pound morning and evening. Somebody suggested a dog tracking dog, and I left a message for the person who did this to phone me back. I also left a message for a Pet Detective agency to phone me back. Somebody also told me during the day that she had spoken to a Psychic who said that Gomez was close to home and needed help to get home.

I stayed out the front of the house with Priya all day, talked to everyone who came, answered questions and suggested what people could do. Each day I told people that they could get Gomez's attention, if they saw him, by using a high pitched voice and by clapping. I reminded them that he was deaf, and that his vision was slightly affected. As the days went on, people shared that information with each other as well. I set up a few chairs out the front, as well as dog treats and insect repellent. It was busy and exhausting, but I felt buoyed by the large response and the positive attitude of people that he would be found. Some people stayed for a while once it became dark, but most left in the late afternoon. Most promised to come back the next day, and Nicola, who I had not met before, talked to me and offered to organise a search party the following morning.

In Nicola's words: *His story just really touched me and I felt I just really needed to help search for him. I think it was his beau-*

> *tiful face to be honest. I couldn't just sit at home and not help out, if it was my pet I would want others to help as well, it was truly heartwarming to see so many people out and about helping look for him.*

When it got dark, I put Gomez's blanket and some food and water at the top of the drive, in case he happened to wander down the road and pick up the scent.

I am a person who likes answers, and it was so challenging not to have any idea where he might have gone. I continually tried to put the known information together in my head, but it was like a puzzle with no answer. If he had wandered down the street, why had nobody seen him? Why was there nothing on any CCTVs? If he had wandered down a steep drive and fallen off the edge, why had we not heard him and why had searchers not seen him. Where would he have gone that Priya decided not to go? Was it somewhere she could not access, or was frightened of? Had he got through an open gate or open door on a neighbouring property and could not get out again? If somebody had picked him up, why was there no information at the pound or at the vets I had contacted? If he had followed a brush turkey, where would that brush turkey have gone? Why was there a poo trail both up the drive and to the locked storage area? Why hadn't there been any sounds from him? It was exhausting trying to wade through the possibilities. And nothing seemed like a clear answer.

I had another sleepless night, trying to will myself to sleep so that I could function well enough to coordinate what was going on, but every time I nearly fell asleep I jolted awake again and checked Facebook, or strained to listen for any sounds which Gomez might have made. My mind could not get out of the loop of endless questions.

At about 11pm I received a message on Facebook Messenger saying that my dog had been found. It was strangely worded:

Hey mate ur dog was found by someone in kandanga.

I immediately messaged back, my hand shaking, asking for more details, as there was no phone number and no details. I had no idea if the message was a prank, or a definite lead. I waited for a response, checking my phone over and over, but I heard nothing until 7am the next morning, when the person who sent the message replied, saying that the owner of the General Store at Kandanga had found my dog. The phone number for the General Store of course rang through for the next couple of hours, until opening time. Why Gomez would be in Kandanga, which was two hours' drive away, was an enormous question. But anything was possible, and it had to be followed up.

Gomez the Puppy

Do not let the innocent and beautiful face of a cream Golden Retriever pup fool you!

Gomez was the most beautiful looking, chunky pup, who I fell in love with on Gotcha day. I had been promised the first pick of the litter, as I had been waiting for a girl for a long time, and once again there was an all male litter. His breeder reassured me that two males would get along well, rather than waiting for yet another litter of puppies. The litter was related to my boy Monty, with many of the same dogs in their line.

My grandnieces and I had visited the pups and had our eyes on a particular one, who seemed cheeky and affectionate. He was assertive and confident. When we arrived for the visit when we would make our choice, however, the breeder told me that the pup we wanted was in fact not available, as she and her fellow breeders had decided that he would be the one to be a show dog. I argued with her that she had promised me the pick of the litter, and we had already started to bond with him. She relented and allowed me to choose him after all, although she was very unhappy with his choice of name, and refused to write it on his papers.

I have always been grateful that I was able to have Gomez for so many reasons, but a primary one being that he had cancer at four years. Had he been a show dog, he would no doubt have been euthanised rather than treated. He was meant to be with me, and I am so glad I fought for him.

Beautiful as he was, Gomez was the naughtiest puppy I have ever had.

He never slept, every day was a different disaster, he pulled so hard on the leash that I developed a rotator cuff injury in my shoulder. He was perfect at puppy school and dog training (showing off), then extremely stubborn and cheeky away from class.

My brother reminded me recently of a party I had not long after getting Gomez, where he ran around my large garden biting every flower off its stem....very pleased with himself!

Some days I would fantasize about a lovely family raising him instead of just me, feeling sure that anybody else could do better than me!

He had no shame! When I came home to a disaster, my old boy Monty would greet me at the door with a look: 'oh Mum, you're not going to be happy...I tried to stop him', and Gomez would come bounding down the hall, with full eye contact and very happy with himself!!! He had no shame.

One afternoon I arrived home to find half the carpet in the dining room pulled up, as he had found a loose piece and pulled it every way he could. He also loved to pull up lawn runners, and my lawn looked like a disaster area. He destroyed all of Monty's much loved soft toys. He found anything that I had put "out of reach" and had a lot of fun destroying it, whether it was the remote control for the television, or my hairbrush.

Gomez had "activities" to play with when I went out, and he was never left for long, as I worked from home most days with some home visits to make on other days. It was amazing how much destruction and chaos he could create in such a short time.

Our vet diagnosed canine Attention Deficit Hyperactivity Disorder, and said I could use medication, or play ball with him every chance I got! I chose the latter and Gomez had a fully committed relationship with his ball until the day he went missing.

A lot of exercise and patience settled him, and from about 2 years old he was perfectly trained and he enjoyed being a well behaved, but cheeky boy.

He grew into such a beautiful boy.

I loved his cheekiness, and the fact that he would "tease" me, even as he became older, for example, giving me the ball, then, with full eye contact, pulling it away with his paw as I reached for it.

But my goodness he tested my patience as a pup.

Monty and Gomez

MY TWO ENGLISH CREAM RETRIEVER BOYS

My old boy Monty had seven years on his own before his life was totally disrupted by Cyclone Gomez!!!

Monty had lots of stuffed toy animals which he loved like a doting parent, carrying them around, sleeping with them and never ripping them.

He retrieved approximately one ball in his life, and when I threw it again, looked at me like I was crazy!!

"Chasing" another dog involved moving his body so he was facing in a different direction.

Going to the beach meant "fishing" in the shallow still water, wandering around and staring down. Occasionally "pouncing", but only once catching a fish under his paw, and looking very panicked before lifting his paw so the fish escaped.

Life for Monty was slow paced, gentle and quiet.

He was an extremely loving, chilled, sensitive, stubborn and happy dog.

Then a little pup named Gomez joined the family!

Gomez had endless amounts of energy...in fact he never stopped, and rarely slept!

He destroyed all of Monty's cuddle toys, pushed in front of Monty, wanted to walk at 100 kph, chased the ball incessantly and retrieved it perfectly. At the beach, Gomez rushed and splashed through the water, chasing all those fishies away, leaving Monty patiently sighing.

Monty was so patient and sweet with his little brother, who was totally inconsiderate of him!!

They could not have been more different. But both were so loving and loveable.

So much love for my beautiful English Cream babies.

Gomez and Priya

Monty lived to just under sixteen years, and Gomez was seven years of age when his big brother died. Although they got along well, Gomee did not seem to miss Monty greatly.

In fact, Gomez quickly took on the role of being the only dog and getting all the attention. He had always considered himself to be wonderful, and now there was no competition.

Mummy all to himself!!!

Gomez and I moved to Melbourne together, and he quickly adjusted to his new life there. He seemed very happy, but the time came when I wanted another dog. SO.... nine months after Monty died.... a little puppy named Priya appeared!

Gomez was shocked!

Yes, he and Mum had visited the puppy a couple of times, but now she was in his home???!!

AND the puppy's name meant "loved one" or "darling".... WHAT?!

And she was VERY annoying....nibbling on his mouth and tail, wanting his food, yapping.....and getting attention!

Gomee looked at me accusingly for the first week or two, as if to say:

'I don't remember discussing this!!!'

Gradually Gomez started to see a positive side. There were more treats around while Priya was learning how to behave, they could rumble together, and she seemed to understand that he was NUMBER ONE! After all, he taught her everything she needed to know. Fortunately, she was wise enough to not follow fully in his puppy footsteps.

He ended up really loving her, and they had a wonderful and fun relationship. They rumbled together every day, even as Gomez aged, with teeth bared and shocking growls and barks, but no blood was every drawn. They loved to play chasings until Gomez became too frail.

As Gomee got older, Priya started to mother him... cleaning his eyes, letting me know when he needed me, giving him more time to do things, even rounding him up at the dog park if he wandered too far away.

Although Gomez was such a self sufficient dog, he did love Priya and liked to be close to her. They both enjoyed being in touching distance when they slept, and Gomez seemed to need that even more as he got older.

So much love for each other.

Day Three

WEDNESDAY 12TH OCTOBER 2022

I woke my family to tell them that Gomez might be with the owner of the Kandanga general store. My son had worked overnight in Brisbane again, but insisted that he would drive there, as he did not want me driving. He was halfway there when I finally had an answer at the store, and a message was sent to the owner. It all took some time, but once I spoke to the owner, he said that he had found a Maremma a few days before, which had since been reunited with its owner. He did not have a Golden Retriever. My son drove back home, and Gomez had not been found. While a part of me did not believe that Gomez would have somehow been taken to Kandanga, I had hoped that it was him. My heart felt heavy and I tried to turn my flat energy into further action to find him.

I updated my social media posts, and phoned the Council pound and the local vets, as I did each morning and evening. I had identified three lost animal sites on Facebook that I posted on each morning and evening, and the posts were shared from there over and over by the community. I also posted on a different community page and the Sunshine Coast Golden Retriever Owners and

Lovers page. Much later on, I found out that a large number of groups had shared my posts on their Facebook pages, having seen my original posts. There were a few which deserve a special mention, being the Sanctuary for Senior Dogs Brisbane, the Spirit of Animal Rescue and the Senior Dog Action Group Australia. These have large numbers of members and their kindness would have made a big difference to spreading the word about Gomez.

Once again people started to arrive at Jarrah Road quite early in the day. The search party was to meet at 10am at my house, and a lot of people had expressed interest in joining. Many of the people who searched the day before came back, and I became aware that they were missing work and other commitments to help search for Gomez. It was strange, however, that many people who had responded to Nicola, saying that they would be there for the search party, did not come. It was not until later that day that we found out the reason.

A woman brought me a beautiful bunch of sunflowers, and I invited her inside the house, so that I could put them in water. She was talking a great deal, generally complaining about her life and her family. I realised that I was not even hearing what she was talking about, as I was preoccupied about Gomez and I wanted to get back outside to talk to any people who had arrived. I suddenly tuned in to what she was saying, as she had moved on from her problems to wondering what had happened to Gomez. She said: *'I don't want to worry you, but I have heard of old weak dogs being stolen to be used as bait in dog fights.'* My stomach did a somersault and I started shaking in rage, trying to control rising tears and horror. I could not believe what she was saying, and immediately asked her to leave the house. I told her that I had been imagining awful things about Gomez, such as that he was injured or had been run over, but I had not thought of what she had suggested, and now that it was said, it would be impossible to get that out of my head. I could not believe her insensitivity, and did not want to hear her apology or rationalisation for saying what she had said.

The pet detective agency phoned me back and told me that they had various "packages" I could pay for, depending on what I wanted them to do. The representative told me that she was happy to have an "obligation free" phone call, which would go over what I had done and what options she could suggest. I explained what I had done and the response from the community. She said that I had already done much of what they would have suggested, but had I thought that he may have been stolen? She knew of a few cases where an old dog had been picked up by a "well meaning person", who had incorrectly assumed that the dog needed care and wanted to give the dog that care at their home. Gomez certainly may have appeared to have been a neglected old dog. He was not wearing a collar, was thin, would have been limping and had stains under his eyes. If he was walking slowly down the road, he might have appeared to have been neglected or even a stray. I said to her that if I came across such a dog I would take it to the nearest vet, and that is why I had been phoning vets in the area. She agreed, but said that some people want to keep the dog, and it seemed possible that this may have happened. The agency could help with such a case by a media campaign, asking people if they had seen neighbours with a new dog, and private detectives if needed. I decided against pursuing that, but thought that it might be an idea to make a video to put on social media, asking people to return him if they had him, as he was so loved, and needed to be home with me. I also thought that I could put a post on the Facebook community page targeting people who might know something. It seemed to me that while I would have paid anything to have Gomez back with me, paying an agency was probably not as worthwhile as making a post and a video myself, given how much social media exposure I already had.

At around 10am, I started getting some messages asking if Gomez had been found, because the posts about him were no longer on the Facebook community page. I immediately checked the page. None of my posts, responses or maps of searched areas were on the community page. None of us could work out what had happened, but over the next few hours, it became apparent that somebody on the page had claimed that my posts were a "scam", and so "admin" for that page had deleted all my posts. Nobody contacted me from that page, and the decision was made on the basis of one person complaining.

There is a history of some missing dog posts being "scams", mainly in the United States, but the wording of those "scams" is quite identifiable. It is unclear how they work, but the aim is to make money in some way. It is also easy to identify the "scams" as the Facebook profiles of the person posting are new and membership to the specific page is very recent. Sometimes the scammer's profile even shows that they are from a different country. I had been a member of this particular community Facebook page since I had arrived on the Sunshine Coast, and had had a Facebook profile for at least ten years. But they still accepted somebody's opinion that my posts about Gomez were a scam.

I was being accused of something that was not true, at a time when I needed all the help that I could get. My chest burned, like my heart was being ripped out, or I was being stabbed. The hope that I was building through the response I had had, was shattered. If people did not see the posts, they would think that he was found, and so they would not help any more. Or they would believe that it was a "scam" and disregard the genuine appeals for much needed help. Numerous people tried to post on that page to question what had happened and the page was inundated with complaints, but as the day went on, the admins for that page would not approve any posts which mentioned Gomez, or which questioned their decision to delete posts about him. Up till then the people searching for Gomez had put all search areas and maps and details on there, and all this information was now lost. This was the reason that not many people had turned up to join the search party, after saying that they would.

After all the posts about Gomez were deleted from that page, I was "blocked" and unable to comment or post on that Facebook page. I asked on other pages if people could complain to the community page, and others contacted me to say that they had already asked what had happened to the posts about Gomez. I found posts on other lost pet pages asking what had happened.

For example:

All his posts have been pulled from the local page. Has he been found? Anyone got any updates?

I have a bad feeling about it. Why not simply tell us all that he is ok.

It seems the (community) page (where the initial posts were done) admin are being ridiculous, thought it was a scam which it isn't and deleted the posts, blocked the owner and anybody commenting on him.

OMG what?!? Why would they do that!!?? What a disgrace!

I saw someone had put a post up earlier asking where they had gone but it had been removed.

Somebody had taken a screenshot my last post on that Facebook Community Page. It read:

PLEASE HELP!

My 15 year old, deaf white Golden Retriever has been missing from Jarrah Road Buderim since Monday.

Experts have suggested to me that somebody may have picked him up thinking he was a stray, as he had no collar on.

If you have seen him or have picked him up thinking he was a stray or neglected, please contact me or take him to the vet, no questions asked.

If you accidentally knocked him down with your car and didn't know what to do, please let me know.

If a neighbour or someone you know has a new dog, or you hear unfamiliar dog sounds from their place, please let me know.

He limps, has stains around his eyes and not much bowel control. Maybe he looked like he wasn't cared for or loved.

Gomez is SO loved by me. I know how to keep him safe and comfortable and he feels safe when he is next to me. I know how he likes to be cuddled and where he likes to be stroked.

He has medicine, injections and pills for his joints, to keep pain to a minimum, eye care for his chronic eye problem. He is seen by a vet every few weeks. I clean up any accidents with no fuss.

Gomez survived cancer at 4 with surgeries and a year of chemo, and another cancer 6 years ago.

He has a little dog sister who loves him, gives him kisses, and they still love to play together. She is so confused and sad.

He loves the beach and dog park and his own special ball (no other ball will do). I know how to make the only sounds he can hear now he is deaf. I take him and his sister out each day.

He lives with me, my 4 year old granddaughter and her parents. The 4 year old is desperate to give him cuddles. She is SO sad.

He is SO loved and SO well cared for, and when he is ready to go, I have a vet who can help him to go gently in my arms, like my last boy.

I hope this will help you to return him, look for him, or to report ANY sighting to me.

Please help – I just need to know.

Nicola messaged me in the afternoon, asking for news and offering to organise another search party for the following morning.

She wrote: *I can't stop thinking of your beautiful boy.*

Luckily other people also messaged me and I was able to explain what had happened, and that Gomez was still missing. Somebody messaged me to say that she had done a Reiki healing session for Gomez by distance, and said that she was sure that he was close to home and still alive.

At 2pm that day, settlement was expected on my house in Melbourne, so I also needed to be aware of messages and phone calls about that.

The man who had the dog tracking dog phoned me back, but unfortunately told me that it was unlikely that his dog could track Gomez after more than 24 hours, so he was not prepared to try. We had a long phone call, and he gave me a great deal of useful information. He asked me if Gomez had a preference for the way he turned to walk when he left home. I said that I had not walked him much since coming to Buderim, as he could not walk far, so I took them to the dog park each day. Occasionally I would take them for a short walk, and we normally turned to the left. As I was answering him, I remembered that in Melbourne, Gomez always wanted to turn left when we left home. The dog tracking man said that it was therefore very likely he had turned to the left at the top of the drive.

He also told me how to create "scent trails" with Priya, explaining that somebody needed to drive me to a perimeter and then Priya and I needed to walk back to the house, dropping treats along the way. The only way we should walk was towards home, so that if Gomez picked up the scent, he could follow the scent trail home without confusion. This meant that apart from everything else that people were doing, I had to ask for lifts several times a day for Priya and myself, as I could only walk towards home, not away from it.

In the afternoon, I was tidying up the flyers on the verandah, and a woman came up to collect some. I am not sure who she was, and do not remember seeing her before then, or afterwards. As we stood looking at the road, she commented on how many cars were coming along the road at speed, as some people started returning home from work. She then said to me that it was possible that Gomez had been run over on the first day, and then dumped elsewhere, as people would want to hide what had happened. I decided to just pretend I had not heard, as I did not have the energy to confront her insensitivity as I had in the morning with the other person who talked about dog fights. The exhaustion and pain caused by such comments is hard to describe, as my mind was already having to process all possibilities.

The neighbour diagonally opposite our house had complained from the first day onwards about so many cars parked on the street. His response to somebody who pointed out that they were parked legally and not blocking his driveway was that 'accidents happen'. He would not give us access to his property to search for Gomez. On Day Two he had sent up his own drone, apparently to interfere with the accuracy of the drones being used to search for Gomez. Kate confronted him regarding his behaviour in impeding the search. Finally his wife gave some people access to look in his property and to determine what the strange noise was from just behind the fence. We had all thought that it could possibly have been

Gomez crying in pain, but it ended up being a piece of machinery he was using.

In many ways, this was the worst day of the time when Gomez was missing. It was so difficult to stay hopeful, and it felt like the obstacles were building up. The false sighting, the new ideas about what might have happened to him, being accused of being a scammer, the deletion of all the posts about Gomez, as well as the loss of important maps of completed search areas, and other information, from that community Facebook page. Time was passing, and if he was lost in the bush, the chances of survival were becoming less with each hour. My energy level, after two sleepless nights and the stress of wondering what was happening to him, was falling quickly, and I felt like the initial surge of adrenalin had dissipated. This was the point where I found it the most difficult to hold on to any hope.

On the other hand, it was becoming clear that those people who had promised me that they would search for him until he was found were determined to do so. So many people just kept coming back and searching for him. They shared the burden with me, the concern about Gomez, the anger at the Facebook community page, the anguish of some of the comments made to me. Kate, for example, was an advocate for Gomez and for me, in protesting to the Facebook page, and taking on the very difficult neighbour who was hampering our search efforts. She argued with him and insisted on finding out what the sound was coming from his property, so I did not have to do that. I realised that I was not alone, and that people genuinely cared about Gomez and about me. I will always be so grateful for that support.

Posts on other pages in Facebook also warmed my heart, such as:

> *Any news yet? Poor wee man.*

> *Oh my goodness, I woke up in the night thinking about him. Hope he's ok and someone has him safe and sound ready to give him back this morning.*
>
> *Me too. He has really touched my heart.*

The balance which occurs in our lives was very clear to me at that time. The challenges were enormous. Nobody had any idea where he would be. He was old and in poor health so was unlikely to survive this, I felt useless as I could not physically search, some supports had been withdrawn, some people had made horrific suggestions as to what might have happened to him. Despite this, I had an entire community supporting me. People I had never met before, apart from one or two, were committed to helping me find my precious boy. That kindness filled and healed my heart, just when it was shattering from the awful experiences of that day in particular. While I have had to do so many things on my own in my life, I did not have to solve this on my own. The people who surrounded me and cushioned me in my pain were going to find him. They were not going to give up.

Just a Dog

BY RICHARD BILBY

From time to time people tell me, "Lighten up. It's
just a dog."
or "That's a lot of money for just a dog."
They don't understand the distance traveled, time
spent or costs involved for "Just a dog".
Some of my proudest moments have come about with
"Just a dog".
Many hours have passed with my only company
being "Just a dog"
and not once have I felt slighted.
Some of my saddest moments were brought about by
"Just a dog".
In those days of darkness,
the gentle touch of "Just a dog" provided comfort
and purpose to overcome the day.
If you, too, think it's "Just a dog", you will probably
understand phrases like
"Just a friend" or "Just a sunrise" or "Just a promise".
"Just a dog" brings into my life the very essence of
friendship, trust,

and pure unbridled joy.
"Just a dog" brings out the compassion and patience
that make me a better person.
Because of "Just a dog" I will rise early,
take long walks, and look longingly to the future.
For me and folks like me, it's not "Just a dog".
It's an embodiment of all the hopes and dreams of
the future,
the fond memories of the past, and the pure joy of the
moment.
"Just a dog" brings out what's good in me and diverts
my thoughts
away from myself and the worries of the day.
I hope that someday people can understand it's not
"Just a dog."
It's the thing that gives me humanity and keeps me
from being
"Just a man " or "Just a woman".
So the next time you hear the phrase "Just a dog",
Smile because they "Just don't understand".

The Community

A post on Facebook stated:

He brought a community together…what a legacy!

Not all of us can do great things, but we can do small things with great love. ~ Mother Teresa

The number of people who responded to my need for help was quite amazing, and far exceeded the normal response for a missing dog. Before and since Gomez went missing, I have not seen such a strong response to a lost dog on the Sunshine Coast. I believe that it was unprecedented. Although I experienced this extraordinary community response first-hand, it has been difficult to understand how it came about. My personal and professional values have always included kindness, generosity and helping others, but I have also been aware that others do not always have similar values. Being able to reach such a large group of people with a similar value system seems both unlikely and even magical, but it happened.

Some people helped directly by searching the bushland, searching down driveways, dropping flyers all over the Sunshine Coast, organising photocopying of flyers, putting up posters, knocking on doors in a 2 or 3 kilometre radius and engaging others to help. Others shared Gomez's story on Facebook and through other social media. Some suggested methods of finding a lost dog, such as dog tracking, pet detectives or psychics. Others used their contacts in radio and television, council or politics to spread the word. Some groups in social media took on his cause, for example, the Facebook site for senior dogs, making sure that all their members knew that a vulnerable old dog was missing on the Sunshine Coast.

Helping others is known to activate areas of the brain associated with pleasure, social connection and trust. Helping others gives something back. Our society has, however, over time become less concerned with community and more concerned with materialistic and more selfish motivations. Many people feel a lack of "community", and this was exacerbated by the isolation during Covid. "Making a difference" can feel impossible as so many of us feel powerless and voiceless. It may be that seeing a lost vulnerable old dog gave people the opportunity to do something to help and to feel that they could make a difference.

Karen, who searched for Gomez, described the feeling amongst the people searching in a beautiful and perceptive way:

> *We kept turning up to search because of some inexplicable unified bond. We would all smile and greet each other before setting off with a sense of hope. Each person there was remarkable. It's not often that people stop their daily lives and just do something for someone...in need, in a desperate situation. Everyone that turned up for Gomez did so with kindness.*

Gomez was a beautiful looking dog, and as he aged, his face was still beautiful, but also vulnerable. The main photo I used on the flyers, posters and Facebook posts was a recent one of his face, looking at the camera. What had originally been a beautiful photo taken of him by his groomer, Simone, took on a different meaning when used to let the community know that he was lost. It seemed to speak to those who saw it, saying: 'Please help find me. I need you.' It reflected what a precious old soul he was. That photo, combined with his description of being fifteen years old and deaf, reached people's hearts. The dark stains down from his eyes looked a little like tears. My sister later commented on the similarity between that photo and the French sad clown, Pierrot, whose tear drop eye was designed to make him look sad, vulnerable and trusting. Was the use of this photo the key to the reason so many fell in love with him and wanted to help?

A few people recently commented on this photo when I posted it again on Facebook.

Kylie: *...the beautiful tear stained gorgeous old man that grabbed us all by the heart strings.*

Alison: *the ... older photo really 'speaks to me'.*

Debbie: *...he looks very angelic and is communicating so much love with his beautiful eyes.*

Jane: *...those soulful eyes looking back at us and he looked so vulnerable. And instantly feeling sad and heartbroken for a dog I didn't know. I also recall feeling compelled to join the search like so many others and what was the start of community dog searches (I had never known of one to this degree before).*

Dianne: *It still brings tears to my eyes and reminds me how desperately everyone wanted you to find your beautiful old boy....what a gorgeous boy he was.*

> **Jasmine:** *I think anyone who loves animals, has (or has ever lost) a beloved pet couldn't help but be drawn in. It was his eyes that jumped out at me - so soulful and trusting. All I could see was his precious little face and those eyes for days and was so worried and upset for him and for you.*

Some people who searched for Gomez told me that while they always shared posts of lost dogs, they had never searched for a dog in person before. They felt a strong pull to help. Many said that they could not explain why they experienced such a powerful emotional response. One person, Aly, told me that she saw the Facebook post in the morning, and then later that day went to the movies. She left the film part way through to contact me, and to offer to organise some search parties. She was unable to say exactly why she had reacted so strongly, but she felt compelled to help find Gomez. Another person, Cayden, told me that he had already searched a few times, but he was at the gym when he realised that he had to return to keep searching. Many said that they could not sleep as they were thinking about Gomez, all alone somewhere. The people who came to help, or contacted me, referred to him in loving terms, such as 'beautiful boy" and "precious soul". They fell in love with Gomez, even though they had never met him.

> **As Kylie put it:** *We never knew your boy but we loved him, he touched our hearts and he broke them. He brought an entire community together and you must be so proud of him for that.*

Many of the people who helped to search for Gomez had a Golden Retriever, and were able to imagine the heartbreak of that dog going missing. Some had an old Golden Retriever or other senior dog.

> **Helen expressed it this way:** *My previous Goldie lived till he was 14 years old and my current Goldie is 11. The thought of*

> *either one of them being lost, alone, hot, thirsty, scared, hungry or hurt was what prompted me to help search for Gomez. I have searched for younger dogs previously but a Senior doggie really hits hard.*

Many had lost their Golden Retrievers or other dogs not long before Gomez went missing, and they were still grieving.

> **As Marni commented:** *I tragically lost my old boy a while ago in horrible circumstances, was not working and just felt an overwhelming feeling of wanting to help. I just wanted someone to find him, for everyone's sake.*

Some felt a lot of guilt as part of their grieving for their dog, and wanted to make a difference in this case. Others were simply dog lovers who knew that an old dog would find it difficult to find his way home if he went missing. But underlying all those reasons, there were so many people who just wanted to help, because there was a need. Some had never had a dog, but could imagine how devastated I would be. Others had a dog go missing for a short amount of time, and understood how unbearable my feelings would be.

> **For example, in Leannen's words:** *I lost an 18 year old blind and deaf silky terrier while I was at work. It was 6 hours from when I got home until I found her stuck in reeds next to a dam. It was the longest 6 hours of my life so I knew just how you were feeling Gwen and it's the worst.*

I experienced extraordinary empathy from the community. So many people said to me that they could not imagine the heartbreak of having an old dog go missing, and for a number of those people, the fact that I could not physically search because of my mobility problems, added to their desire to help. Nobody who came to help made any judgement. Nobody asked me why I had not double checked the garage door. While I judged myself harshly, the people who came to help understood that accidents happen, and they just wanted to help find Gomez and to get him home.

The number of people following Gomez's story on Facebook grew rapidly with so many people sharing his story, and Facebook being flooded with posts about him. It seemed like he was on every Facebook community page and on all the lost dog sites. I also played a big part in this by updating posts morning and evening, and personally greeting and thanking everybody who came to help. I tried to respond to every message on Messenger and every comment on Facebook. I also decided to put up stories and photos about Gomez on Facebook, so people could get to know him, and knew how loved he was. I have included these stories in this book. The community started to fall in love with Gomez, and with me, as they could see our bond from the posts, stories and photos. A strong commitment grew to getting Gomez home, where he would be safe and comfortable. This commitment was expressed in different ways, depending on how people were able to help.

> **As Sharon put it:** *I'm an animal lover and Gomez really touched my heart. I was drawn to him. I was unable to help in the search due to working an hour away. I continually shared the posts to get the word out so more people could help. My nephew lives in Gomez's street so I contacted his family who were also taken by Gomez and helped in the search. My nephew's wife was a member of this group. Being a young working family they may not have the time to be on Facebook. I am intuitive and felt a deep connection to Gomez and then what I call the Gomez Family, who all worked together to bring him home, spread some light in tough times. With Covid, homelessness, cost of living soaring etc, it was such a sense of community for Gomez.*

Nannon is an example of somebody who could not physically help with the search, but was touched emotionally and determined to spread the word and make suggestions.

In her words: *I originally saw a post in the Sippy Downs Community page. A poster of Gomez with details about his age and being deaf. I immediately felt a connection to him and the need to try and assist where possible. I went to the group page which had recently been set up and tried to help with getting the word out by sharing the poster and offering suggestions to help. My dog had recently died unexpectedly and I was dealing with feelings of grief, guilt and shock. That night I could not sleep thinking about poor Gomez missing and the tears would not stop. The next couple of days I continually checked the Gomez search page hoping desperately that he would be found. I was not able to assist in the search as I have young children at home, but I tried to do what I could behind the scenes. Those days I was an emotional wreck, and I could only imagine what you must have been going through. As I continue to struggle with my grief and guilt of my loss, I see these wonderful posts in the group that remind me how lucky we are to have these beautiful creatures in our lives who will forever be a part of our family.*

Catherine also helped in the same way: *I wanted to join this group because all throughout the time Gomez was missing, I shared information and posts on social media because I felt helpless not being able to actually look for him because I'm in Brisbane. I loved him even though I had never met him. This group reminds me of this darling beautiful boy and how much others also love him. I loved him because we have 2 senior Goldens, also his photos.*

As did Jo: *I have a beautiful goldie and she is my world. Living in Vic I couldn't help you search but I joined for moral support, prayers and positive vibes. I must say that I was uplifted by the*

> *amount of love and support this group has shown. It's really shown the best of humanity.*

The commitment to find Gomez was reinforced through the community, as it became something so very important to each person helping. There were so many people giving up their time and promising to keep searching, and that motivated others to give their time and develop a strong commitment to finding him. People came back again and again, taking time off work and from their families to help somebody they did not know to find a dog they had never met.

Within the large group of wonderful dog lovers, there was a smaller group with the ability to think like an old dog and to work out where he would have gone, and for what reasons. While we had no idea where he had gone, these people were able to ask the questions which gave them some clues to rationally work it out. Karen, for example, saw a brush turkey when first talking to me, and asked me if Gomez had any interest in them. When she found out that he had developed an interest through the fence, this helped her to think through how that may have played out. Thinking back on Gomez going missing, it now makes perfect sense to me that he saw an opportunity to chase a brush turkey up to the locked door and then up the drive. Then most likely into their nest in the bush at the top of the driveway. But at the time he was missing, my mind was so full of possibilities that I did not have that clarity. Fortunately, there were people there who had that clarity and could follow it up.

Whenever a loved dog goes missing, it is so difficult for the owner to think clearly. Emotions are in the forefront, with grief, fear, panic, guilt and horror leading the charge. Add lack of sleep and that person's cognitive skills are greatly impacted. In retrospect I can see that we could have found Gomez much more quickly if I had gone with one possibility rather than multiple possibilities.

My first thought was that he had fallen down into the brush turkey nest at the top of the drive, where Priya whimpered. When he did not respond on that first day, I dismissed that totally, attributing Priya's whimpering to her (and my) anxiety. This is the reason that most owners cannot find their dog on their own. Firstly, most have no experience in looking for a lost dog. Secondly, they cannot think straight and need others who are not being led by their emotions. Many owners of lost dogs tell me that they have searched everywhere, but they have not been able to tune into the mind of their dog and work through the possibilities in a methodical way. They need help from others who can do that more easily. If a dog is possibly in the bush, it is so easy to miss it, and having people look with fresh eyes and from different angles can make all the difference. It is generally extremely difficult to find a lost dog who cannot find its way home, unless the owner is helped by others.

I am in a community choir and recently we sang "Lean on Me" in harmony. The words resonated so strongly with me! If we need help or we have a burden we need to ask for and accept help. My life as a Social Worker had involved working with others, as a "helping professional", but I had never been that good at accepting help myself. There are times when we need to ask for, and accept help, and what I discovered is that there are so many wonderful people who are right there, ready to give it. It was an amazing life lesson for me, teaching me that I could rely on others and not have to shoulder the burden on my own. I now know that if we ask for help, there are going to be people who give it freely and with love and kindness.

The community who came to my aid in searching for Gomez had a lot in common with me. Usually when we interact with others in society, we are interacting with people who have different values, attitudes, beliefs and experiences to ourselves. Somehow I was able to reach a large group of people who loved dogs, had empathy for old dogs and valued them, and who cared deeply about the suffering of an old dog lost in the bush or somewhere else. No doubt many of the community had different values and beliefs in other areas, but in terms of committing themselves to searching for Gomez, they were very similar to me, and took on my cause with open hearts and strong motivation. There is something so wonderful about people who genuinely love dogs and other animals.

The people who came to help met other people with open hearts and similar attitudes to themselves. They found themselves amidst a group of dog lovers who were doing all in their power to bring a vulnerable old dog home. This reinforced their motivation to find Gomez. They came together and encountered the heartfelt efforts of each other. They formed a team of like-minded people with one goal in mind. To find Gomez. Many started referring to themselves as "The Gomez Crew", and the core group have continued. Others have joined "The Gomez Crew" since that time, even though they were not involved in searching for Gomez. Many have remained friends since this time, and many have become my own very wonderful friends.

Special mention needs to be made of the people who came back day after day. Jenny was involved from the first day that Gomez went missing, as I had already met her briefly beforehand. She lived over the road and had a sweet little dog called Rusty. She was out the front of her house when I discovered that Gomez was missing, and immediately started searching nearby properties and alerting neighbours that he was missing. She continued to do so every day, and was a constant for me in the midst of so much chaos and fear. She is a wonderfully warm and generous person. Jenny had great empathy for me and was a source of comforting hugs and offers of cups of tea. Rusty was a senior boy, and she could imagine the dreadful feelings that I was dealing with. She has remained a beautiful friend for me and has supplied much of my new garden.

Whenever I see Jenny, I feel a strong warmth and connection from her, and I will never forget her kindness.

> **In Jenny's words:** *Gwen, there is just something so very unique about this lost dog story & that would be that it was Gomez & you.*
>
> *Having only met you Gwen, Gomez & Priya in our street once we chatted about our senior dogs & how precious & loved they were.*
>
> *My heart jumped in my chest when I heard of the afternoon that Gomez was missing. So many people from all over the Sunshine Coast came & helped in the nights & days of searching.... there was an overwhelming feeling in the community's spirit to find Gomez & return him to Gwen & family.*
>
> *I am very proud to have been a very small part of the awesome team of people that were part of Gwen & family's search for Gomez.*

Suzanne arrived the day after Gomez went missing, and like so many others, was there every day after that. She is also a very warm and caring person. Suzanne has a gorgeous little Jack Russell cross, Sammy, and has had a Golden Retriever in the past. She immediately knew how awful it was that Gomez was lost and could imagine how she would have felt if it had been her dog. She bonded straight away with Priya, and Priya found her to be a source of comfort as well. She and Jenny searched a lot together and formed a bond. Suzanne often took me to the end of the roads with Priya to make scent trails back to the house.

Dave arrived on the first day, having sent me a message that he was on his way with a drone and his dog. He arrived with his older dog, Tom, and a thermal drone. He used the drone each day, but was also honest with me about its limited use in the thick bush and tall dense canopy. It did give a perspective of the old BMX tracks through the bush and where there was water. Not only did he use the drone, but he searched the bush. His sister, Kylie, joined him most of the days, and they were among the people who told me that they would continue to come back until Gomez was found.

Dave has an enormous heart and an enormous love of dogs. He has two black Labradors, Tom, who is getting older, and Indy, who started her life with a different family and is now lucky enough to live with Dave. Kylie, like her brother Dave, has an enormous heart. At the time of the search she had one golden Labrador, Leo, having lost her other golden Labrador, Jack, only a few weeks before Gomez went missing. She was, of course, still grieving as Jack had been her heart dog, and she missed him dreadfully. Both Dave and Kylie had loved senior dogs and knew the pain I would have been going through. They fell in love with Gomez and were determined to help. They also both felt a strong affinity with me, and have remained friends. I see Kylie regularly and just love the warmth and connection we share. Our dogs are best of friends, and Kylie now has little Daisy, a beautiful golden Labrador and sweet little sister to Leo. Kylie has written an account of her experience in searching for Gomez, which is included later in this story.

Again, I often wonder where these beautiful siblings came from. How very lucky was I that they chose to help me when I needed help so badly. I will always be so grateful to them both, and will treasure my ongoing strong friendship.

Donna and Kate also arrived on the first day, and then searched in the bush every day. They brought Kellie with them a couple of times who was a dog “expert”. Donna and Kate had always had Golden Retrievers and had two at that time, as well as a rescue Staffy. They have always loved dogs and knew Golden Retrievers well. There is no way that they wanted Gomez to be missing or in the bush for any length of time. They understood his vulnerability and the urgency of finding him.

I know that Donna and Kate wanted to be the people who found Gomez. They were so invested in finding him, and would do whatever was necessary. They went deep into the hostile bushland and came out each day with leeches, ticks, scratches and snake sightings. They brought a wonderful positive energy to each day, and I felt sure that if anyone found Gomee, it would be them. Donna and Kate came back each day, and said that they had understanding bosses. I was concerned that they were missing work and income in helping me, but they dismissed my concern, showing such a strong commitment to finding Gomez.

Julie arrived with Sharene the first morning after Gomez went missing. The two of them were fully invested in helping and supporting me in finding Gomez, and both offered invaluable help. Julie has not maintained contact with the group, but I will always be so grateful for her compassionate and generous help when I needed it so much.

Karen searched for three days, and has an uncanny ability to work out how a dog thinks. In this case, an uncanny ability to understand an old dog, and work out where he would go and how he would behave. Karen asked me a lot of questions about him, his temperament, his interest in the bush turkeys and his current health and mobility. She has had dogs all her life, and understands the bond we have with older dogs, and the end of life plan we must have. I will be forever grateful that she understood him (and me), and could see how he had become lost, and work out where he would have gone. She was able to become so well attuned to him, and formed a special connection. He needed her to do that. Karen was determined to find Gomez.

In Karen's words:

I am an animal lover and basically keep on social media like Facebook for the lost pets...

Usually just to press share to get the image of the lost pet out to others that just may recognise the lost pet.

I have great faith that especially dogs can make their way home by scenting, so I don't jump onto the go and look straight away wagon.

Old dogs that have lost senses and have mobility issues I keep a special interest in and try to follow to see if they make it home.

They may need help to get back home.

Why ?

Because I was so very fortunate to grow older with a 17 year old cattle dog, a 15 year old collie rough and a 16 year old Jack Russell. Every person whom has reached this stage in a pet's life has formulated "a plan" .... A what if the day comes that I say goodbye.

We plan the last meal - (cooked chicken, pizza or cat food- in my case. Each special and highly prized by said pet).

Daily assessment of the walks, dog's mobility, getting to the toilet, bowel motions, peeing etc.

It's all done silently and discussed at length with other family members.

We gaze into our happy old hound's eyes and try to see answers to unbearable questions.

So when I hear of an older dog going missing- I watch.

For Gomez it was his eyes, the persistence of the posts (how much it was shared) and I knew the terrain.

So on day two/three I said to my husband we needed to help.

When we got to the house I absolutely knew Gomez needed to be brought home.

I knew his mumma had her plan.

So I was so sure this old boy had not gone off to die .... I thought he was just on a "miss adventure". One that he couldn't physically get back home from.

So I personally searched knowing what little I knew (poor mobility-loved to chase and was just beginning to become curious at the scrub turkey)....so each day I searched for an old boy who was going to try his best to get back home.

It was important for this last journey- last plan to be done.

Each day I became surer that he was down the hill and following the gully (unfortunately there were so many). Each day I prepared a little more to go into the gullies a little further and I put more into my backpack to get him home safely....

It became so much more than a search.

It was a meeting of like minded souls that had the purest of intentions.

It was a show of compassion, love and humanity at its best.

I was proud to be amongst the search party.

Evan and Brigitte were probably the first people to arrive, on the evening that Gomez went missing. They were warm and compassionate and determined to do all that they could to find him. Evan and Brigitte gave me hope on that first night that people would come to help.

In Brigitte's words: *I got a Facebook notification on my phone and saw it as I was about to leave my dance class and drive home. When I arrived home I showed Ev the post as soon as I got to the door and straight away he said 'we need to go look for him.' We got in the car and drove straight to your house. I grew up with Golden Retrievers and Evan and I have two golden retriever boys of our* *own. The photo of Gomez had a huge impact on us. We could tell that he was a beautiful, sweet, special old boy. I can't remember what you wrote on that post, but I felt your love for Gomez and how out of character it was for him to wander off. We also thought about how we would feel if it was one of our goldies, and how we hoped people would help us. Golden retriever owners are good people and a special community.*

Brigitte also added that after they spoke to me they went to the nearest garage to buy a good torch and looked in the bush, down driveways and around nearby streets. They could not stop thinking about Gomez, and the next morning Evan searched for about four hours behind the property. When he was found, Evan said that he could not believe how far Gomez had managed to go in the dense bush.

Jamie also arrived on the first night, and he and Jenny searched upper areas of the bush with their ute lights and torches. I could see people in the bush, and only found out later that it was them, along with Evan and Brigitte. Jamie came each day with his drone. He was very honest about the fact that he could not search in the bush, due to his fear of Australian snakes, spiders, ticks and leeches, but made sure that he was busy searching all areas which he felt he could handle. What a fantastic young man, here from the United Kingdom and ready to help and be part of his new community.

So many people felt that they just had to search for Gomez.

In Sharon E's words: *My daughter and I felt like we had to help search for Gomez because we could not stand the thought of him being out there by himself. His age had a lot to do with it, we wanted to see him home, warm, dry and safe. It simply broke our hearts to know he was lost in a strange place and away from his family who obviously loved him so much.*

Aly and Nicola also warrant special mention as they gave up their time to organise search parties, with neither having done that previously for any other missing dog. They also used contacts, for example, Nicola organised the ABC radio interview. Helen organised the interview with Steve Dickson and was also responsible for an extensive Twitter campaign. Karen P, Cate, Jilly, Nikki, Jane, Narelle, Kate, Sharon E, Dan, and Sony Lee are a few more people I remember helping over that time.

> **Jane's words are representative of what motivated many people:** *Always had and loved dogs. I would hate mine to be missing not knowing where they are or if they are ok. If I see dog missing near me I will go for walk around the streets. In the case of senior dogs like Gomee and Lilly who were missing in bush areas I feel compelled to look further knowing unlike a younger dog they probably aren't going to travel as far and need more help to get home, and while a dog missing in a very residential area has a far greater chance of being noticed by a resident or someone walking, these pups need people to actively search. Greatest reward is knowing both dog and owner can be reunited. It always makes me happy to see posts where dogs have been found, especially when they have been missing for more than a day.*

> **Similarly, Karen P commented:** *Gomez's lost dog message came up on my FB feed one day and I was instantly keen to help - I think firstly because it was distressing to read his age and being deaf, that the location was only a 10 minute drive from where I lived and that I loved goldies (we had one when I was a teenager and I still feel sad when I think of it!).*

Not everyone is mentioned here, as there were hundreds of people involved, helping in so many different ways. I did not meet them all, and many searched without making themselves known. My memory of who I met is also still a blur. There were friends and family interstate who supported me through the ordeal. There were also people I had never met, who did not live on the Sunshine Coast, who supported me and followed the story every day. Those who shared his story ensured that he was well known and encouraged others to volunteer to help. What I do know is that everybody who searched or helped in any way, made it more likely that Gomez would be found. It was an incredible community effort and every individual brought hope, love, commitment and energy to searching for Gomez.

I have so much love and gratitude for the people who helped me.

Sharene

Sharene and Julie arrived the morning after Gomez went missing. Both came ready to help for however long they were needed. I had never met them before and they did not know me or my boy. They were there each day, helping to coordinate, copying posters and flyers, talking to volunteers, following up on crank calls, and basically supporting me in whatever way they thought I needed. This was done face to face, through Facebook Messenger and by phone. Although I wanted to know everything that was happening, I know that Sharene and Julie sorted out some problems between themselves, so that I was not bothered.

Sharene has remained involved since that time and has become a very dear friend. She has the most beautiful open heart, and is such a humble and warm person. Sharene is simply a "good" person, who is soft, sensitive, loving and generous. She lives with the grief of losing her last precious dog, Trixie, and this seems to have made her even more sensitive to the feelings involved when a dog goes missing. Like Gomez was to me, Trixie was Sharene's heart dog. She no longer has a dog, no doubt because losing Trixie affected her so deeply. She minds two dogs as needed for friends, and loves any contact she has with dogs.

Sharene loves my Priya, and would have really loved Gomez. She had a Golden Retriever some years ago. Sharene is one of the very few people I would trust to care for Priya when needed.

When I first met Sharene, I was impressed by her organised approach to knocking on doors with flyers, and her commitment to helping in every way that she could. I had no idea just how much help she would be and how she became such an integral part of the whole search effort and my life from that time on. I must say that I often wonder where such people come from. I needed somebody like her to help me to get through those days, and there she was. How does that happen? I did not even realise how much I would need her. She has been like an angel for me, as if she was sitting on my shoulder, telling me that things would work out, and that she was there to help.

A remarkable gift for which I will be forever grateful.

Gomez and his Ball

Gomez loved his family, food, his ball and the beach, but not necessarily in that order!

When Gomez was diagnosed with canine ADHD as a puppy, my options for him were medication or lots of ball chasing! I chose ball chasing, and Gomez chose to develop a passionate relationship with his ball.

My first retriever, Monty, thought that it was demeaning that I threw the ball and expected him to bring it back. He did it once in his life, and then looked at me with disdain when I threw it again. Priya, my third retriever, will retrieve the ball, but is highly distractable, and so it is often me doing the retrieving or searching for the ball. Gomez, however, knew what his name meant.... 'I am a retriever and I retrieve beautifully'.

Gomez always had an orange and blue "chuck it" ball when he went to the dog park or dog beach, even as an old doggie.

He absolutely LOVED his ball and was totally committed to it. He could recognise his ball from other balls which looked the same to anyone else. To a silly human, it might look exactly the same, but he knew its history through its smell and feel. He knew HIS ball, and could usually find it if it did go missing. If he could not find it immediately, he would search and search until he found it.

As a younger dog, Gomez was quite athletic and would leap for his ball, anticipating where it would be in the air and where it would land. Whenever I took a video or photo of him chasing his ball, he would look directly into the camera. So proud of himself.

As we neared the dog park or dog beach each day, he would increase his pace to get there so that he could play with his ball. That was his goal and it made him so happy. It was definitely a love affair.

But, with such love, also came heartbreak for poor Gomez.

There were the temporary losses which came when his beloved ball rolled out of reach under furniture, or was so far under a shrub in the garden that he was unable to get it. Gomez who had gone through cancer treatment without a cry or fuss, would cry and fuss until I somehow managed to get the ball and give it back to him!

Then there were the permanent losses of his beloved ball.

When I lived in Sydney, I used to take him and his brother Monty to a beautiful South Coast spot called Currarong.

There was a channel from the surf to the lagoon which had a very strong current when the tide changed.

One day I threw the ball in there for Gomez to retrieve, not realising that the tide was changing.

Gomez was a fast swimmer, and as the tide went out, he tried to get his ball, but it was moving too fast.

I could see him tiring as he continued to chase it through the surf and out to sea.

Of course, I was screaming like a mad woman, but he took no notice!

Finally, he heard one of my many loud 'STOP' commands and turned around, eventually getting back to the beach, absolutely exhausted!!! I thought that I was going to lose him that day.

Another time, his ball went under the fence next to the railway line, too far in to be reached; and another time it sank so deep into smelly mangrove mud that even Gomee could not retrieve it.

A couple of times, other dog parents insisted that his ball belonged to their dog, despite my protests and arguments that Gomez knew which one was his ball. Gomee was left with their dog's ball, which looked the same, but was a very poor substitute.

I knew his immediate grief, and I also knew he would not accept another ball easily. If I threw it, he would run, sniff it and leave it! Plus look at me accusingly, wondering why I was not throwing HIS ball.

So, to get him to accept a new ball, I had to put it next to him while he slept, put it in his food bowl, put it in his mouth again and again, until after a few days he finally accepted it. During those days, he was miserable when we went out, forever looking at me with tragic eyes and wanting me to find the real ball!!

So much love for my quirky beautiful boy.

Gomez: The Surfer Dude

Gomez loved the water, and did not need the gradual introduction to swimming and the surf in the same way as Monty and Priya.

He took to it immediately, and he could not get enough of it. He was not afraid of it at all, and even tackled the open sea, the day his ball was swept out by the tide.

Not only did he love the waves crashing in the surf (again unlike Monty or Priya), but he became very confident in catching big waves into shore.

Perhaps in the beginning he loved the surf because he wanted to retrieve his ball, wherever it went. That overcame any fear he may have naturally felt. Or perhaps, as an adventurous dog, who was up for anything, he loved the feeling of the water and the waves.

Whatever the reason, he was a wonderful strong swimmer, and the sea was probably his favourite place to go. When we arrived in Melbourne and stayed at Black Rock, he did not mind the very cold winter water at all, and learnt to dive in from the side rock wall.

As an older dog, Gomez was more wary, as he became a little unstable on his legs. He only went in the shallow water, and gave up swimming in the deep or going into the waves. Instead he would do more digging on the beach, and seemed very happy with that option.

So much love for my surfer dude.

Gomee's Magnificent Tail

Gomez's tail was magnificent and always amazed me. It was quite bouffant, and he often received compliments from people, or glares from jealous doggies.

His tail went everywhere he went, but also had a mind of its own.

It could knock things off coffee tables with a quick swish, was just the right height to brush across the face of a child, sleeping mum or another dog, and when wet, could wet everything around it.

Occasionally it would be full of leaves or cut grass and left a trail of debris, and sometimes it was pretty muddy....well you know the rest!

Like all dogs, Gomez was sometimes surprised by his tail, and looked at it like he had never seen anything like it!

So much love for that magnificent tail.

Gomez's Great Love of Mud

... THE JOY OF A GOLDIE

Gomez loved smelly mangrove mud!

When we lived in Sydney, we lived in Marrickville, close to the Cooks River. We walked along the Cooks River each day. The Cooks River is not the cleanest river in Australia, and is mostly edged by mangroves and thick, smelly and oily mud. Oh how Gomez loved that mud at low tide! He had a way of rolling in that mud, like a pig wallowing in mud. He felt every delicious oozy part of it, and could spread it all over his body. If I could entice him out of the mud quickly, he would end up half black and half white, but if he refused to come out for a while, he would end up totally black.

Gomez also absolutely loved mud puddles!

When I first moved to Melbourne he came in the car with us for house hunting day trips, as I didn't want to leave him at home alone in an unfamiliar place. One day we stopped at a park part way through our house hunting, so he could have a little run. Of course he found a mud puddle which we hadn't seen. This smelly mud monster shared the car with us for the rest of the day!

At my local dog park in Melbourne, there were several areas which would become large muddy puddles when it rained. At first, before we were well known there, people would call out to me to let me know that Gomez was in the mud. My nonchalant response probably puzzled them, as for me, it was much better than the stinky mangrove mud of Sydney. Just as well people loved him, as he often encouraged other dogs to join him.

Getting muddy most days until he was very old, Gomez was used to being washed with a cold hose. He would stand still without a leash while I washed or rinsed him off, and would turn around when I said ‘turn around’, so I could wash the other side. No warm baths for him!

The joy of Goldies!

Gomez and his Sticks

When outside, Gomez always had a ball or a stick in his mouth.

Chewing a stick was a very serious commitment for Gomee! Several criteria were involved in his choice of stick:

- from a gum tree or a jacaranda
- not too small and not too big
- chewable into small pieces
- crisp and brittle, not bendy
- no splinters

He would then find exactly the right spot to lie down and give it his full attention. The end result was lots of small pieces of stick which he spat out as he chewed.

I always thought that he could have got a job with a tree mulching company. He would not stop until he was satisfied with his work.

When Priya came along she tried to copy him, but often swallowed pieces instead of spitting them out!

As Gomee got older his teeth were not too bad, and his vet thought it may well have been his (rather compulsive) stick chewing!

My funny boy!

Day Four

THURSDAY 13TH OCTOBER 2022

I had another restless night. The nights were so difficult, as I was on my own, and my emotions were so raw. I tossed and turned, cried, checked Facebook every time I "woke", listened for Gomez and imagined different scenarios of what had happened to him. I was exhausted, both in mind and body, and I could not focus easily. I was overwhelmed with everything that I had to do, including making scent trails at every opportunity with Priya. My body could not keep up with the demands placed on it, and I felt like my mind was overloaded. I have always had a vivid imagination and have been an "overthinker", and I could feel these being negatives for me at this time. My heart was hurting continually, I felt guilty and I was grieving for my precious boy. The thought kept coming up that Gomez was too old to be away from home for this long, and that perhaps he was lying dead somewhere. I wondered if the people searching thought that he was still alive, or if they were beginning to think the worst. I knew I was too afraid to ask that question.

My granddaughter did not come downstairs to ask if Gomez was back that morning. It was too long for her, and her initial hope had dissipated. She knew that a lot of people were searching for him, but it must have felt like such a long time for her.

Priya is an anxious dog, and always has been. She was picking up my emotions and was naturally confused by all the activity and different people at her home, coupled with Gomez not being there. I did my best to reassure her, and tried not to get too upset when close to her, but she stayed very close to me. It was difficult for me knowing that Priya was having a hard time as well, as I had to make sure that she was okay. She had only ever known life with Gomez, and it must have felt so strange that suddenly he was not there. I really felt for her and knew that I was preoccupied with trying to find Gomez, and so not very "present" for her.

People have asked me how I kept going for so many days. My answer was that I did not have a choice, as I had to do everything I could to find Gomez. I only know that I was driven by the love I had for Gomez, the fact that he was my heart dog and the fact that he needed me as an old boy. If I had not had the support from the community, I am not sure that I could have kept going, but the support that I received felt so inspiring and filled my heart. The hope that others had, and their determination to find Gomez, helped me to keep hoping and to keep going.

Much of what happened over the time that Gomez was missing is a blur. I remember parts of it, but other parts are impossible to recollect. I imagine that without discussion, my son and daughter-in-law picked up the things that I normally would have been doing around the house and with my granddaughter. They would have seen that I was functioning on a very different level, and that it was impossible for me to leave the area close to the house and do anything else. I had to be there in case he was found, or suddenly came home. It was difficult for my family to suddenly have people in our space, but they accepted that this was being done with kindness and a desire to help find Gomez for me. I know that my son and daughter-in-law would have been also been focussed on making sure that my granddaughter was okay.

My son was also worried about me and the impact of this stressful experience. Several times over the days he commented that he was unsure how I would be at the end of it. He could see that I was just keeping on going, but he knew that it would take its toll. He was absolutely right to worry, of course. I was very aware that as an older person I was not nearly as resilient as I used to be. I do remember, however, being keenly aware that if Gomez was never found, I would not recover. I knew that I had to know what happened. We had bought a house in Golden Beach, and were moving there in six weeks. How could I move away if he was not found?

The legal side of buying our new home did not stop because Gomez was missing. We had conference calls to get through to work out some legalities, and we were working out finances, as well as dealing with the conveyancers and real estate agents for the new home and my home in Melbourne. My son was also still trying to sell his place in Melbourne with a frustrating lack of success. I relied on my son to make sure that anything I was signing was correct, as it was so hard to focus on anything but Gomez.

When all posts about Gomez were deleted on the Facebook community page on Day Three, I felt extremely deflated, as did everybody else involved. So many people had an enormous commitment to finding Gomez, and we all knew that this had really set us back. I decided that the only thing to do was to set up a Facebook page myself, and contact as many people as possible, asking them to join the group and share its existence. My son helped me to set it up, and I messaged everyone who had already been involved, asking them to join the new group, and to let other people know about it. I named the page “Searching for Gomez”. I also posted on other Facebook lost dog pages, and other Facebook pages where Gomez's story had been posted, asking the community of dog lovers to join the group and share the name of the group with others.

> *Gomez has been missing from 31 Jarrah Road Buderim since Monday afternoon. He is 15 years old and deaf. He is a white Golden Retriever.*
>
> *So many volunteers have searched on foot and with drones, letter box dropped, door knocks. Locals have been asked to search their places.*
>
> *Gomee's mobility is limited, so he couldn't have gone far.*
>
> *Somebody may have taken him in thinking he was a stray, as he limps, his eyes are stained and he had no collar on.*
>
> *He is SO loved, and I make sure he is safe and comfortable. I know what he loves.*
>
> *We need help, but ..... community board have just taken down all posts and I cannot post or comment.*
>
> *People are probably assuming he has been found, but he hasn't.*
>
> *I have set up a new Facebook page, "Searching for Gomez". Please join and share to others.*

People started to join "Searching for Gomez" quickly, and by the end of the day the new group had several hundred members. I decided to ask Sharene and Julie, the two women who had been involved from the beginning, to be "admins" for the page, as I knew it was going to be too much for me to manage on my own. While we had lost valuable maps of areas searched, people started to post new maps and information on the new page. I felt confident that nobody could shut that page down, and while we had had a setback, we had to keep moving forward. I also started to put up little stories and photos about Gomez. I thought that it was important for everybody to get to know Gomez better. With other social media posted by the community, the membership of the "Searching for Gomez" page was up to 1,500 members by Saturday 15th October. The page ended up being the best possible thing, and it still exists with over 1,100 members.

After such a difficult day on the Wednesday, things started to fall into place on the Thursday. Time was moving on, so the concern for Gomez's welfare intensified, adding to the urgency. Many people who had been following his story, seemed to make a decision on Day Four that he was not going to find his own way home. They came to help along with those who had been there from the beginning. There were so many people offering help. The search took on a new dimension with search parties organised and less of an ad hoc approach.

Many of the people searching for Gomez were in touch with each other, either in person or on Facebook. They compared notes, drew attention to areas which they felt needed to be searched more thoroughly, put maps up of where they had searched and hypothesised about where Gomez could have gone. It became a full time job for many of the people helping.

So many of the people helping were thinking about Gomez all the time, and trying to get on to his wavelength. Many asked me more about him and wanted to get to know him. I became aware of how much people who had never met him were falling in love with him. He had a huge fan base. The energy being put into finding him was amazing. He would have been found so quickly if that was all it took. The pure intention, high motivation and strong love for him reflected how much everyone wanted him safely home.

People had also contacted radio and television stations, and announcements were made on a couple of stations, ABC, 92.7fm and SEafm, as well as community radio. People searching and dropping flyers in the industrial estate below, told me that people working there knew that they were searching for an old white Golden Retriever, as they had heard about him on the radio.

Despite the concern about how long Gomez had been missing, it was a good day. It was a day full of hope and increased activity to find him. It was a day that new people, who had been following his story, decided that they had to help search. He had been gone too long. Perhaps being shut down by the Facebook community page had ended up being a good thing, because people were angry and motivated by that. The fact that it led to the wonderful "Searching for Gomez" page was beneficial in that everything was in one place, events could be organised on the page, and I could start putting up stories to help people to connect further with Gomez. It was a day when I really understood the positive side of social media, with more and more people sharing and spreading the word, in a way which would not have been possible a few years before. In the local area, the "old fashioned" methods of posters, flyers and door knocks ensured that everyone in the street and nearby streets were aware that Gomez was missing, but when social media was added to that awareness, it was incredible. Everyone on the Sunshine Coast seemed to have heard of Gomez, as I gradually found out over the following months as people recognised his name and knew his story.

Gomez and Cancer

Some of you have heard about, or would have read about Gomez getting cancer at 4 years of age. He was diagnosed with an intrapelvic infiltrative lipoma, a fairly rare malignant cancer which is jelly like and wraps itself around the internal organs. It was affecting his bowel and was quite close to his liver, kidneys and spine. My regular vet, Peter, operated, but closed up quickly saying that there were no visible margins to the cancer, and he would need to be seen by a specialist. Peter was visibly shaken and upset when he had to tell me the news. I was so lucky to have such a beautiful person as Gomee's vet. Gomez had two more surgeries at the Animal Referral Hospital, one from his belly and one from the back. The veterinary oncologist at the Animal Referral Hospital, Tony, then said that they could trial a new chemotherapy, with no guaranteed results.

A few people at the time disagreed with my decisions. They thought that it was too much to put him through, and too expensive, but he was a young fit dog, full of life, so it seemed to me that the only thing to do was to give him a chance. He could not fight it on his own, but I was confident that with expert veterinary help and an environment of love, he might make it. If he had been an older dog, or a dog who did not have such a strong spirit, I may have decided differently.

Treatment at first seemed to be successful, but after a year the growth came back. When that happened, I was told that Gomee would only have up to 3 months to live without further treatment. There were other treatments that they could try, such as radiation therapy in another state, but I felt that he had had enough.

I was heartbroken, but decided to give Gomez the best 3 months any doggie could wish for.

Beach holidays, lots of walks and ball play, all the food he wanted, and of course, lots of cuddles, tummy rubs and very few rules.

I also disregarded some rules in the local area, and let him chase balls "off leash", while keeping Monty on leash. Inevitably I was approached by a council Ranger one day. He pointed out that the park we were in was not "off leash". I told him that my understanding was that legally a dog had to be "under sufficient control", and that Gomez was well trained. Thankfully Gomez remembered his training and came to me straight away when I called: 'Gomez! Look! Come!', so the Ranger was immediately impressed.

I then told the Ranger that Gomee only had a couple of months to live, and that I had decided to just give him the best life during that time. I told him that there was an article written about Gomez by a pet journalist, Caroline Zambrano, if he wanted to look at it. The Ranger was sad about such a prognosis for a beautiful young dog, and said that he would tell the other Rangers to let Gomee be "off leash" in the Marrickville area!! Not just because he was dying, but also because he was well trained and not causing any problems. What a lovely man!

About 9 months later, the same park officially became an "off leash" dog park, and the same Ranger saw me there one day. He remembered us, and said that he thought Gomez had only had a short time to live. I said to him that it was true, but that Gomee was defying veterinary opinion and was going very well. I really hoped that he did not think that I had made up the story, but he was genuinely happy!

So many people cared about Gomee when he had cancer, and his recovery against all odds was always a miracle which did not make sense to the vets and veterinary oncologists.

Gomez and Chemotherapy

As you all know Gomez had chemotherapy for a year when he was four to treat a very nasty cancer.

I suspect the treatment changed the malignant intrapelvic infiltrative lipoma into a benign tumour in the same spot, but the reasons the vets came up with were in the realm of a miracle. On his fifteenth birthday, a milestone for any big dog, I emailed the vet and veterinary oncologist, as I had every year on his birthday, and they rejoiced in his longevity. Tony said one time how delighted he was to be wrong!

The decision to help him to beat cancer was one of the best decisions of my life.

But it is easy to gloss over what a year of chemotherapy is like for a dog. We all know that it is awful for humans.

Gomee never complained, and took all the medication like a trooper. Each time he went to the Animal Referral Hospital for blood tests, ultrasounds or check ups, he ran in to say hello to everybody. They all loved him. But at home, I could see that it was difficult for him at times. He often went off his food, lost energy and slept more. He tired more quickly chasing the ball. His beautiful thick coat lost its shine and thickness, making him look like a brown dog, as it became “see through” when he was wet. I found a photo recently which reminded me of that.

When it regrew, his coat was curly for about six months.

As you also know, Gomee was a hyperactive dog as a pup, with boundless energy and not much need for sleep. His treatment slowed him down, but he probably still had more energy than most other dogs his age.

At times, I wondered if it was fair to have put him through the treatment. After all, he had no say in the decision! But his young age, his extraordinary zest for life, and his trust in me, had persuaded me. We were so lucky that it was the right decision and it gave me so much treasured extra time with him. He not only survived, but was very healthy for his age.

My beautiful brave boy!

Day Five

FRIDAY 14TH OCTOBER 2022

I woke from another fitful night of worrying about Gomez and what could have happened to him. My level of exhaustion was something I had never experienced before. The only way to keep going was to find an "auto-pilot" level that we all have deep down to access in a time of trauma. My body felt heavy and it was getting more and more difficult to put one foot ahead of the other, and the thought of doing more scent trails with Priya was really daunting. My mind did not seem to have any more capacity to take in any further information, or to make any sense when I spoke or tried to think something through. My emotions were overwhelmed and I fluctuated from wanting to cry and lose hope, back to my known strengths of determination and moving forward. My heart hurt.

I knew that I had another big day ahead of me, and that time was becoming an enemy to an old lost dog. Part of me had started to hope that somebody had taken Gomez into their home, and that they would see sense once I made a video showing that he was so loved. The alternatives were too difficult to contemplate. How could he have survived in somebody's yard, under their house, down a hole in the bush, or trapped somewhere, for this long? How could he still be alive with no pain medication, and the dangers of ticks and snakes, if he was in the bush? The weather was starting to warm up, with a top of 25 today, and he still had his thick coat, which was due to be clipped that week. There had not been a single sighting of Gomez, so we were still no closer to working out where he was.

I updated all my posts on Facebook and noticed that more and more Facebook pages were putting up posts about Gomez. Today I noticed that Golden Paws Rescue had posted about him being missing. Each time somebody posted about him, or shared posts, it multiplied the chance of him being found. I am still unaware of some of the people and groups who helped in this way, as it was done with quiet compassion. I put up my morning post on "Searching for Gomez":

It's Friday morning and Gomez is still missing.

This is what we did yesterday:

Created this page ("Searching for Gomez").

Blasted .... community board until anything about Gomez was allowed back on.

Messaged and texted everyone with details of this page.

Put details of this page on numerous sites and updated those.

Phoned vets and pound and looked at their Facebook pages.

Radio stations were contacted, but not sure which ones.

A number of people searched bush and area physically...details in other posts from yesterday.

Gomee's groomer, Simone, from Mooloolah Valley, put flyers everywhere she could think of between here and there.

Some doorknocking was done with flyers.

Drones searched again.

I laid scent trails with my other dog.

Please comment or post anything I have missed.

Today:

Volunteers are meeting at 10am here at 31 jarrah road to coordinate another search.

More flyers have been printed and will be here for anyone who can help.

Someone is doing larger posters to put on posts.

I will do new scent trails with my younger dog.

People are coming this morning to video a live feed re efforts to find Gomez. It would be great to have as many people as possible out the front at 10, even if you have to head off later.

Please don't be put off if you don't want to be filmed...they can accommodate that. Thanks Bobbie Bendy for organising this!

Please comment or post with any other plans for today.

THANK YOU EVERYONE.

When I look at that post now, I marvel that I was able to think clearly enough to put a few words together.

A local politician arrived at 10am to do an interview with me, which he then shared on his popular Facebook page. One of the volunteers, Helen, knew him and had organised this. I gave a heartfelt interview, probably far longer than he expected where I pleaded with people to help or to give Gomez back to me if they had him. Looking back at that interview, I could tell how emotional and exhausted I was, just by looking at my face, but surprisingly I still made sense. How amazing our coping strategies are. Both my family and my professional background had enabled me to be able to switch into problem solving mode quickly and to speak clearly on topic. It was like a switch went on, and I realise now that every time I had to talk to somebody about what was happening, I was able to use that strategy, without even realising. I was in physical and emotional pain, and that was evident to all around me, yet I was still "coping" and "functioning".

> Kylie later wrote to me in Messenger that:
>
> *Honestly Gwen you were so amazing and strong despite how incredibly hard your situation was. It was clear for the world to see that your heart was breaking and you were so stressed....but you pushed through that, showed your love for Gomez and made yourself vulnerable. You accepted all the help and you were so very brave and present through it all. You were the face and voice for your boy.*

I am so grateful that I was somehow able to do that for my beautiful boy.

So many people joined the search organised by Aly that day. People seemed to feel that it was a critical day, and the strong commitment already there multiplied in an extraordinary way. New people who had been following his story from the beginning had come the previous day, feeling that poor Gomez obviously needed help to get home. Facebook was buzzing with posts and Gomez's Facebook page was full of comments as the membership grew. I am not sure how many people joined the search that day, but the core group who had been there from the beginning, with people like Donna, Kate, Suzanne, Jenny, Sharene, Julie, Dave, Kylie, Nicola, Jamie, Dan, Evan, Brigitte, Cate, Kerry, Linda and Karen, were able to give information to the people who joined the search. It seemed like a huge number and an enormous amount of hope and energy, with people ready and determined to find Gomez that day. Helen came from Brisbane, having been a support from Day Two. She went into the bush to search, and also organised the video interview at 10am. She had also started an extensive Twitter campaign. Membership of "Searching for Gomez" reflected this, with people joining from overseas and all over Australia.

I made a short video and put it on Facebook. It was a heartfelt plea for anybody who had Gomez to please give him back, similar to the Facebook post I had put up a couple of days before. I told of my love for Gomez, and the care and attention which he needed and I gave him.

As with other days, searchers went into the bush, went down driveways, knocked on peoples' doors again and put out flyers. Several of the very steep driveways close to us were searched many times. I believed that it did not matter how many times the same place was searched, as if he had fallen off the edge of a drive, into a hole or thick vegetation, he could be seen by somebody looking from a different angle, or he may have slowly moved since anyone had looked in that area. Priya and I greeted everybody we could out the front of the house and also made a few scent trails. Somebody brought chicken to be taken when searching, and for the first time since Gomez went missing, Priya seemed happy, as she kept getting small pieces of chicken through the day. Priya had been very quiet and confused all week, and was staying very close to me. We had been together all the time as I was worried about her.

It was also increasingly difficult for my granddaughter, as she was confused and sad. She loved Gomez, and could not understand how he could just disappear. She spent time with Priya and I out the front on the days that she was not at kindergarten. I was at a loss for what to tell her, and had to just keep hoping that Gomez would be found so that she would have closure. I knew how much I needed closure, whatever the outcome, and imagined it was just as important for my granddaughter as it was for me. If his death was the outcome of this horrible week, I was also starting to dread the impact his death would have on her, as her first significant loss.

At 5pm I received a phone call saying that my dog was in this person's backyard, but they did not know if they could keep him there. The male voice was strange and his comments were vague and unhelpful. He said that he had seen a poster and this was the same dog. He finally answered my question about the appearance of the dog. My question was 'what colour is the dog?' He answered 'Brown.' 'But the poster has a photo of a white dog!'. 'Someone coloured in the one I saw.' I asked him where he lived and he did not seem to know, but finally gave me an address. I spelt it out to double check. 'What is your name?' I asked. He answered 'Tom', and then I decided to ask his age, to which he answered '14'. By this time, it obviously seemed like a crank call, but I asked him to try to keep the dog there and my son would go to the address. My son drove there straight away, but there was no house at that address. I let Sharene and Julie know, and they checked the address and thought that it may have been a genuine call, but the address was a little wrong. They met up and drove to the alternate address, but nobody there knew anything.

A reward was discussed by a few people helping to search for Gomez, and the idea of a "Gofundme" page was raised. I did not want to offer a reward, as I thought that we would then get a lot of crank calls, and I was also still feeling wounded from the accusation of my posts being a scam. I believed that offering a reward might start that rumour again, and preferred not to have any money involved.

In the evening I updated all my posts as usual. I asked for help with some tasks the next day, and my beautiful grand-niece, Rachel, who lives in Sydney, offered to help with emails to local vets. During the time Gomez was missing I had received a lot of phone calls from people, as my number was on all the sites. This evening I received a call from somebody who at first said how sorry she was about Gomez and that she wanted me to know how many people cared. She then went on to talk for a long time about her own experiences in the past with losing dogs. This was not the first time I had received a call like this, which started off with sympathy for my situation, but developed into a caller needing emotional support for his or her own situation in the past. This was exhausting for me, and perhaps because of being a Social Worker, it seemed that I somehow encouraged them despite trying to get off the phone. While I would normally have a lot of time for anybody who needs to talk, this was not the time for people to try to get sympathy from me. I had nothing left to give.

I went to bed with mixed feelings. It was a long time now, and it was becoming less and less likely that he could survive on his own. It was becoming so exhausting to keep up hope, yet so many people were involved, with numbers increasing every day. I had to borrow their hope and I also had to keep hopeful for Gomee's sake. If I let my energy fade, he might somehow sense that I was giving up. I had to remain strong for my boy, and hope that miracles can happen.

Gomez's Careers

I'm not sure if many of you know that Gomee had a few careers during his long life....champion ball chaser (athlete); surfer dude (athlete); mulch maker (gardener); general duties of checking on those around him and guarding the house (good boy); finding those who needed emotional support (therapist); food tester (usually unasked); supervisor of younger dogs' behaviour (bossy boots manager); and wannabe dog model (show off).

But he also had a very important job at any beach he visited...

as an engineer.... rearranging sand into amazing channels for the water.

He would dig and dig, with great purpose, until he was satisfied with what he had achieved.

He would then drop his ball in the channel, and watch what happened, rescuing the ball if necessary.

Such a clever good boy, with such a strong work ethic!

Gomez's Bromance

Very few of you would have known that Gomez had a beautiful bromance with a kelpie named Jack about 7 years ago.

Both loved the ball and would chase together and then find a spot to lie close to each other. They reminded me of two guys going off for a smoke, excluding all others. Close to each other, but not talking much.

When Priya arrived, they were both rather put out that she wanted to join their little ritual. She was like the annoying little sister, and if she lay near them, they would somehow agree to simultaneously move away to another spot, leaving her all on her own. Priya persisted, despite the initial undisguised rejection, and she was finally accepted.

Jack's dad, Louis, was disappointed that Jack did not like the water, so I suggested that Gomez might be a good role model in that area. So one day we met at Port Melbourne, where Gomee convinced Jack that water, especially when combined with a ball, was super fun!! Jack enjoyed the water from that time on.

Ah....the special love of a bromance!

Day Six

SATURDAY 15TH OCTOBER 2022

I "woke up" from another fitful sleep, noticing that I was no longer listening for Gomez. I somehow sensed that if he were still alive, he would be too weak to make any sound. I could also feel myself coming to terms with the possibility that this was now a "retrieval" search, as it was unlikely he could have survived this length of time, particularly if he was in the bush or outside anywhere. If he was in the bush, he was exposed to the elements, the heat, ticks and snakes, and it was doubtful that he had found water or food to sustain him. A voice inside my head wondered how much pain an old dog could endure before just giving up. I knew Gomez would wait as long as he could for me, but he was old and weak. I felt an overwhelming sense of sadness that morning.

Nicola had organised a phone interview with an ABC radio journalist, who was very responsive. Unfortunately, I cannot remember her name. I also received an email from the animal communicator who I had contacted a couple of days before. She is very well known and respected, and I knew how important any information was for the people searching.

I updated all my Facebook posts and posted on "Searching for Gomez":

Good morning you wonderful people

Today a group is meeting here at Jarrah road at 10am to door-knock and search in the bush. Wonderfully large group yesterday worked hard to find him, but no sight or sound.

I made a short video trying to reach someone who may have taken him. Any other ideas on how to reach someone who took him to "look after him" (this has happened in the past with old dogs), please let me know.

So today we have:

- The organised 10am group, and like all other days I'm sure people will come when they can.
- There is a huge box of flyers here.
- I have just done a phone interview with ABC news.
- I have just received fresh info from an animal communicator who has been helping: 'he is under a tree and asked me for healing which of course I did. The ground is a clump of old trees and rather wooded and there is a pond near by. I told him you will be looking for him today and your searchers will be guided to him. This is obviously very urgent. Amanda'
- My grandniece in Sydney is emailing all local vets with a photo. They have been phoned previously.
- I am physically going to the council pound.
- I will continue to make scent trails with my other dog, as advised by an expert.

- Please wear suitable clothing if you go into the

bush...snakes, ticks, leeches, overgrown weeds and steep drops. Don't want any of you to be lost or injured.

- At 31 jarrah we have chicken to take with you, dog treats, and also have insect repellent.
- Also be aware that if he is seen or heard to not rush him, but to sit, with chicken or treats, so he knows you're not a threat.
- There are also some areas which people think need more intense searching, so we'll discuss that at the 10am group.
- People have already posted today with ideas so pls check posts below.
- Thank you everyone and please comment with ideas or anything I've forgotten.

Aly had organised the 10am search as an "Event" on "Searching for Gomez", and it was also in my updated posts on other lost dog sites. An enormous number of people turned up before 10am and through the morning. Word about Gomez had spread everywhere, and people were now certain that he could not find his own way home, or he would have done so already. This was the sixth day of him being missing. It was also a Saturday, so on top of the people who had been searching all week, and the others who had joined them later in the week, there were many new volunteers who had not been able to search through the week because of work.

For example, Linda: *I joined the search on the Saturday..... While closely following it throughout the week, every time I looked at the beautiful pictures of him my stomach turned to knots knowing that he was somewhere and in much need of our help. I have a 16 year old girl who we found abandoned as a puppy and have lost her a few times over the years. I know the pain you feel when they're out there lost.*

> **And Nikki:** *I had a strong feeling that morning he would be found on that day so I came up .. my 3yr old needed a nap so decided to drive him to your place and drove around looking.*
>
> **Karen P commented:** *I had seen your desperate cry for help each day on a number of different notice boards - I felt your pain. Your determination to find Gomez made me want to help you. To add to this, I'm a massive dog lover so always worry and head out sometimes when a dog has been advertised as missing on group pages to add to the search party.*

There was high energy and a strong determination in the air. I am sure that I was not the only one who was thinking that he could not have lasted this long, but this was not mentioned, or at least, not to me. Aly organised people at 10am, and as had happened on other days, maps made by people who had searched were shared with new people. There had been a lot of communication between people all week, with people suggesting places to search. Often a single person had got to a spot and had not been able to search further, so they would share this information on Facebook, suggesting that more people look there. A lot of people searching through the week talked of a "strong feeling" that they were close to Gomez but did not find him.

Aly had commented on the "Searching for Gomez" page about the bush, as so many people had no idea how treacherous it was until they were in it.

> **She posted:**
>
> *For anyone who searched the bushland, you know what it was like. The ticks, snakes and leeches are the absolute LEAST of your concerns. It was thick, dense false ground hollows, utterly dangerous for falls and the ground required long sticks for prod-*

ding and often times a machete to clear.....Thank you to everyone who risked their own wellbeing to search that forest.

Sharene and I tried to ensure that everybody who went into the bush went with somebody else, and was aware of the dangers. We had become increasingly worried that somebody would get injured, and had decided that we would not let people search the bush if they were not properly prepared, but we had no real control, with many people just taking off without talking to us first.

I have vivid memories of some of the people who searched that day. More vivid than on other days. All the people who had been there from the beginning were there, with their wonderful commitment and hope. I remember seeing Karen C, who had been coming for a few days, and who coincidentally knew one of my Melbourne friends. We had found that out when she had looked at my Facebook profile on her way one day, and had realised that we had a mutual friend. Karen paired up with Cayden who I remembered from one or two times before. They headed off with great purpose and with bags full of essentials. They said that they were going deep into the bush again. I also remember meeting Jackie for the first time, and thinking that she had such a positive attitude and the fitness to go with it. We wanted people to go into the bush in pairs if possible, but the only person left to pair Jackie off with, at that time, was the woman who had talked to me for so long on the phone the night before. It did not seem like a good match, but there was nobody else at that time.

Everybody headed off into the bush or down the road. There was an energy about the day. It felt like a critical day, and everyone was far more serious and purposeful than before. I kept thinking about the words of the animal communicator and hung on to these words for hope. If Gomez was waiting and expecting people, as she had said, perhaps he would find the energy to make a noise or be seen. I was discarding the idea that somebody had taken him, and seemed to have finally settled on the idea that he was in the bush somewhere.

People kept arriving and some took off doorknocking. I answered the many questions which came up and tried to persist with a hopeful energy. All these people were giving up their time and risking their safety, because they wanted to find Gomez. Again, I felt humbled, grateful and amazed at the wonderful people who came to help.

At around midday, Janine and David arrived and asked what they could do. Suddenly Sharene shrieked out; 'He's been found!!' She was on the phone and I could not hear what was happening on the other end. She kept giving me bits of information, the most important being: 'He's alive!!' I could not believe it. Everything that I had been hoping for, but it was completely surreal, like a weird dream in slow motion. Sharene asked if somebody could drive us down the hill, and David volunteered. They rushed off without thinking towards the car, and I called out: 'Wait for me!!!' Everyone was in shock. I had Priya with me, and asked Janine to mind her.

Karen, Cayden and Jackie had found Gomez about 230 metres down from the house, near water. He had not turned to the left when leaving the driveway, but had turned to the right. It would appear that he had fallen into the bush at the spot where Priya had whimpered on the first night. It was a thick area with a brush turkey nest, full of debris, and a steep decline from the top area. It made sense that Gomez had chased a brush turkey up the drive, pooing with excitement and movement as he went, and had then fallen down into the nest following the bird. The brush turkeys may have attacked him, as they do at nesting time, or he may have lost consciousness from perhaps hitting his head. For whatever reason, when we looked with Priya and called him, he did not make a sound and was not visible from the top. Or perhaps he had already tumbled further down the steep hill at that stage, and could not hear us that night, because of his deafness. Once Gomez was able to move again, he would have no doubt tried to climb back up, but was limited by his mobility. The only option for him was to keep moving downhill, in the hope that he could somehow get home. Some of the way he would have tumbled at steep declines due to his increasingly weak legs. So many people had searched that area, and yet nobody had seen him. We will never know the reason for that. I know that some of those people have found it very hard to accept that they may have missed him earlier in the week.

David, Sharene and I headed off down the hill in David's car, with Sharene still on the phone. It was probably best that Jackie had phoned Sharene, when she thought that she was phoning me, as I was not functioning. I could not even work out where we were going, but we ended up down in the Kunda Industrial Estate. The wonderful people who had found Gomez decided that they could only get him out of the bush if they went downhill, as it was so steep. They told Sharene that they could see a sign of a smash repairs yard, and were going to come through that. We found it, and David parked nearby. It was early Saturday afternoon, however, and the yard was locked up with barbed wire, padlocks, and possibly electric fencing. We rushed down the footpath, finding that all the businesses were locked up for the weekend. David phoned a friend who owned a tyre business there, and he agreed to give us access, and told David that a couple of his employees were still there. They let us in, but when we looked out the back of the workshop we realised that there was no way that Gomez could be carried through from the bush, as there was a huge ditch out the back with a steep drop.

Gomez had been found, but it now seemed impossible to carry him through to safety. How were Karen, Cayden and Jackie going to get him to us? While we were searching the street, Sharene was trying to talk with Jackie to work out how they could get Gomez out. The phone cut in and out, and it started to feel like there was no way they could. It was difficult for us to identify landmarks from the road which they could recognise from the bush behind. We also kept calling out and listening for them. I remember gazing up into the bush, trying to see some sign of them. Gomez was found and I was desperate to see him and tell him that everything was okay, but it became more and more unlikely that they could get through the Industrial Estate, and we really did not know what to do.

There was a big purple building in the middle of the block, with a sign saying "NIGHTCLUB". We suddenly realised that it seemed to be open. Not a nightclub at all, but a business servicing people all day and all night. We went to knock on the door to ask them if there was any access. David said: 'I've never been to a brothel before!', and I remember Sharene saying something like: 'I'm sure these are special circumstances!' Luckily the manager told us that the three rescuers could bring Gomez through there. At last! We had a way of getting him through. Now we had to communicate this to Jackie and they had to identify it from the bush. At least we could laugh a little at this bizarre situation.

Someone back at the house had a contact at the Tanawha Emergency Vet and told them that we were coming. Julie was putting up a post that Gomez had been found, and people were responding in large numbers, excited and amazed. There were 470 reactions and 260 comments just on one of these posts. This is what so many people had hoped and prayed for. It hit me that whatever the outcome, it would affect not just me and those who knew and loved him, but all those who had come to love him over the last few days. There was an enormous emotional investment in Gomez being found and surviving his ordeal.

After what seemed like hours, Cayden, Karen and Jackie carried Gomez through the purple brothel on a makeshift stretcher. I rushed to him and touched him, and my precious boy lifted his head. Perhaps he wagged his tail... I cannot remember. It was obvious that he knew it was me. I could see how weak he was. The days in the bush had ravaged his frail body, and his beautiful white coat was covered with poo, weeds and dirt. The three rescuers put him carefully in the back seat of David's car, and said that they would see us later. Sharene got into the very back section of the car, with no seatbelt, and I got into the front passenger seat, making sure that I could reach around to keep touching Gomez. I was crying and shaking with joy and also shock at how he looked, but somehow it did not occur to me at that time that there was a chance that he would not survive. He had waited to be found and had survived his ordeal. He knew I was with him and kept lifting his head.

My precious boy!

They were waiting for us at the emergency vet, along with a small group of people who had been involved in the search from the beginning. The nurses gently took Gomez out of the car and started to carry him in. I followed them and said that I needed to go in with him. I assured them that I would not interfere, but that I had to be with him after all the time he had been away from me. They allowed me to go in while they started examining him and hooking him up to various monitors. I had my hand on him, but made sure that I was not in the way. I am so grateful that they allowed me to go through to the examination room with Gomez.

It's so difficult to describe my emotional state in that room. I think I was in shock that he had finally been found, and also some denial at the state he was in. From the moment that they started to examine Gomez, however, I could see that there were major concerns. It was not until then that I thought, for the first time, that if Gomez was found, he might not make it. The vet with the stethoscope kept checking and rechecking, and then said something quietly to one of the other vets. I noticed that he could not move his legs, which to me was not surprising after the amount of time he had been lost. The vet kept checking reflexes, however, and looked concerned. It started to dawn on me that it might not be the happy ending that I and everyone else had hoped for, that is, of getting Gomez home where he belonged. It then suddenly hit me that it did not look like he was going to make it. I felt light headed and fearful all of a sudden, but of course wanted to be strong for my boy. My tears were welling up and I wanted to protest loudly that he was okay. How could the trauma of the last week end with him not making it?

The vet said that they had made him comfortable with some medication and asked that we talk in another room. I went through and a nurse told me that there was a group of people outside the vet waiting for me. I remember Sharene, David and Julie looking shocked and upset when I told them that it did not look like good news. Julie told me that my son and granddaughter were on the way to the vet, and to wait for them before anything was decided.

I went back into the room where I was to talk with the vet. I asked her if we could wait a few minutes for my son and granddaughter to get there. She agreed. While I waited, I quickly posted on the "Searching for Gomez" page:

> At the emergency vet. Vitals are not good, particularly heart, lack of sensation in legs.
>
> Just about to talk to vet about his condition.
>
> Even if he doesn't make it, we found him.

> Will keep updating but first....you are all so amazing and this outcome is a miracle.

My son and granddaughter arrived and the vet spoke to us in the back room. She pointed out how much damage Gomez's time in the bush had caused. His heart was very weak, and she said that even if they could get him through this period, it would remain weak, and he would not have long to live. She said that it was amazing that he had survived this long at his age and in his condition. His legs were not responding to stimuli and his reflexes were gone, so it was unlikely that they would recover, given that they were weak before all this happened. The vet added that he had maggots through his body and in his matted fur and these would have been attracted to the poo and other dirt on him. She had not checked for snakebite or ticks, as there was so much already going on for him.

I sat there listening to her talk and it was again like an "out of body" experience. My beautiful boy was not going to make it after all. I felt so very sad but also relieved that I could be with him at long last. If he had to die, he would die knowing how much I loved him, and the horror of the last week would hopefully dissolve for him.

The inevitable and compassionate decision was for Gomez to be euthanised. The vet said that they needed to prepare Gomez, and left the three of us in the back room while they did so. My son went to pay the bill, and I had a chance to talk to my granddaughter about what was going to happen. This was going to be her first major experience of loss. She had always loved Gomez so much, and he had been such a sweet gentle boy with her. She knew that he needed care and was thoughtful and kind with him. But losing her much loved Gomez was going to be so hard. I told her what was going to happen, and that Gomez would be helped to die so that he did not suffer any more. They would give him an injection and we could talk to him, feed him chicken and stroke him until he died. I told her that while he had got very sick in the bush, he had waited to be found so that we could be with him when he died. She and I both shed tears as we thought about what was going to happen. Such a very sad outcome. But so much better than the other possibilities of what could have happened to Gomez. And so much better than him dying alone, wondering where I was.

The vet took us back into the surgery and Gomez had been cleaned up a little and covered with a purple velvet blanket. How very appropriate for such a special boy, whose collar and lead had always been purple. How had they known to do that, given that he had not been wearing his collar? It would have been more perfect if we had been at home, but given that this was happening at the emergency vet, we could not have asked for more. He was lying there peacefully, regal and dignified. He had been given a sedative. Gomee responded to our touch and relaxed even further. The vet gave us some shredded chicken to feed him, and despite being heavily medicated and close to death, his retriever appetite gave him the energy to eat it enthusiastically. We stroked him and told him that we loved him. I thanked him for the wonderful years that he had given me, and hoped that he could forgive me for not being there for him during those five days. He drifted off and made his way to somewhere he could run free and feel young again.

Everyone who has loved a dog and has had to make the decision at end of life knows that it is the worst day. Nobody who has been through this ever forgets it, and some people can never contemplate having another dog after such intense heartbreak. To face such a horrible decision after searching for Gomez seemed to make it even harder than it had been with any other of my very loved dogs. To have lost him, and then to have to lose him again seemed unbearable. I had dreaded the last day as Gomez aged, knowing that my heart would never be the same when I lost him. How right

I was. It has never returned to how it was before, no matter what I have done to remember him and to remember the love we shared for fifteen years.

It breaks my heart when I hear that dog owners cannot bear to be with their dogs when they are euthanised, because it is too painful for them. So the poor dog spends his last moments with the vet and vet nurses, who are caring, but are not the ones who the dog needs. It is something that we need to do for our precious dogs so that they know how loved they are as they die. We are so loved by our dogs and the least that we can do is to show them our love during the difficult times. One of the most heartbreaking times of a dog's life for the dog's owners is this time, but we owe it to them to be there for them. At least I was able to do that for my precious boy, Gomez.

It was definitely not the outcome that I had hoped for. I wanted my Gomez back for the time I had left with him. I had been cheated of the last few months or year of his life. The fact that he had survived on his own for so long meant that he had not been ready to die. The vet said to me that he was obviously very strong to have survived. But Gomez decided to go on an adventure and could not get home. If it had not been for the massive community effort, he could not have held on much longer, and he would have died alone, feeling like nobody cared. If he had not been found I would have always wondered and grieved for him, not knowing what had happened to him. He was found, so I was able to be with him, and I knew a little about what had happened to him. I will never be sure how he ended up where he did, but once we knew where he was found, it made sense. Whatever the reason for his decision to go into the bush, he could not get back out, and so he just followed the steep contours of the bush, sniffing out water, and possibly feeling the vibrations of the industrial area below. The distance Gomez covered was quite surprising, but I believe that he was trying to get home in the only way he knew.

Sharene wrote on the group page:

I will never forget that day either. I was the lucky one to get that phone call that day and yes I yelled that out. It was like an out of body experience and I can just remember Gwen's face. The adrenalin was pumping for sure. As I keep saying there was a reason everybody didn't stop searching after 6 days and that was for Gwen to see Gomee once more.

I know personally what kept me going and continue to search and do whatever I could to help was putting myself in Gwen's shoes. I had my cocker spaniel go missing overnight and I will never forget the pain and anguish I felt just for that short time. I can't imagine what Gwen was feeling I will never forget receiving that phone call to say Gomee was found. I will also never forget the ride in the car to the vet. All Gomee wanted was Gwen's hugs and kisses. I will never forget it. I am very grateful for the new friends made for life (albeit would have preferred under different circumstances).

We left the vet and drove home, stopping on the way for my son to remove some of Gomez's missing dog posters. There were still some people at the house. Everyone was in shock, and some were particularly hard on themselves, believing that they should have searched different areas. I tried to reassure people that they had done everything that they could, but some people, like Kate and Donna, had been there every day and had invested so much in finding him. They all wanted to bring Gomez home, and they did not want the outcome that occurred. To me, each and every person who had been involved was responsible for finding him, whether they had searched directly, shared posts or contacted a radio station. It was a beautiful and massive combined effort.

It had been an extremely difficult day for me and my family, but also a very difficult day for the enormous number of people involved. When he was found, there was so much happiness and excitement for those there at the house, and for everybody following the story. It was beyond belief that this massive community response had resulted in finding Gomez alive. One of my friends told me that she and her family were in the middle of having a celebratory lunch for Gomez being found, when they heard the news that he did not make it. It was a day of highs and lows.

The grief felt by everybody was palpable. How could he have been found and then not survive his ordeal? How could this be the outcome of the beautiful effort made to find him? Everybody's hopes and dreams of finding this beautiful old soul were shattered. A lot of tears were shed at the news. Those directly involved were shattered, and it was also very difficult for the three people who found him.

Very quickly after Gomee was found, people started to ask in person and on Facebook about where he was found. It was so close to where others had searched. A few mentioned that they did not go any further, when they were very nearby to the spot, as they could not work out how Gomez could have gone any further. Many expressed the wish that they had found him earlier for me.

The end of the story is tragic, and not what anybody wanted. But the truth is that all the efforts made and the love for him led to Gomez being found on the 6th day. He was still alive, as if he knew we would find him. He lifted his head and wagged his tail when he was found, as if to say: 'Finally.... I knew you would come....'

My brave boy hung on against all odds and could not have lasted much longer.

I may have given up hope if so many people had not been there with their hope and determination.

After I posted the RIP Gomez post, people started to see that, given the outcome, the most important thing was that I was with

Gomez when he died. This is what I have focussed on. The 'what ifs' and 'if onlys' are too difficult to deal with. I was with Gomez when it truly mattered, and he knew he was loved. What more can we offer our precious dogs?

Since Gomez's death, I have become aware of a number of people who never found their lost dog, and never knew what happened to their pup. I have no idea how people can cope with that. I know that I would have found it unbearable to never know.

First Hand Accounts

OF CAYDEN, KAREN AND JACKIE

I asked the three wonderful people who found Gomez to write their own accounts of that day.

CAYDEN

Gwen, I've been wanting to write down what happened for a long time but I always wanted to save it for when you asked me – so it can be as raw and real as possible.

I think it was the Wednesday or so when my partner first sent me an ad for Gomez missing, as I usually do I went on the ad and had a look into it. I'm not sure what happened but I just felt an instant connection. A few months prior I had lost my long family dog Rex due to old age, and then a couple of weeks before my own dog Zephyr went missing for about 15 minutes – which was a terrible feeling.

I think this was on a Tuesday or Wednesday, as I was sent this during work so I wanted to go and have a look and see if I could help. Mind you I have seen hundreds of ads for missing dogs yet I haven't ever gone out and looked for them – this one was just different and I couldn't explain it.

My partner and I took our Kelpie Zephyr to the area just behind your house and looked around for about an hour. I didn't feel like we were close but I felt like I needed to look anyway. I just couldn't stop thinking about Gomez and also yourself – in not being able to at least have closure if the worst had happened. It stuck with me throughout the night as I was reading everyone else's comments and efforts and I felt like I needed to have another look.

So on Thursday morning before work I searched again. It was quite early at like 7 or 730 and I had another look for around an hour – I ended up going a bit further into the bushland and found a little clearing spot with a big tree – I felt something different about this spot and I think it was because one of the Psychic ladies or healers who posted in the group sort of described an area like this where Gomez was around – so I had a look around this area for about 15 minutes but then headed into work. I thought I had done all I can and exhausted all options.

I was reading the comments and posts in the group to search for Gomez constantly – but I knew there was a search group on Saturday Morning. I wasn't originally going to go – as my partner had work and I had searched for the last 2 days – yet I remember the exact moment where something changed. I was at my gym Club Lime in Maroochydore in the morning and I was on the Cable Machine doing Triceps Extensions, and I just felt something come over me. I immediately left the gym and came to help look – and I got there just before everyone was starting to leave the house to search. Everyone was pairing up and Karen looked like she was pretty geared up – she asked if I was willing to go right into the thick of the bushland which I was – so we teamed up and went down. We searched the same areas I had searched closer to the house because we were sure Gomez couldn't of gone that far due to Arthritis and his old age. After an hour or so we decided to work further down. We ended up in that same clearing spot with the big tree and I felt some kind of calmness or so. I let Karen know about this spot and also brought up about the Psychic Lady who described a spot like this.

At this point Jackie then stumbled into the same area – so we all decided to keep looking. We worked our way towards a creek near the top of the bushland and stopped. We were considering turning around and coming back – yet I think Karen said she was going to explore a little further down. So we all decided to search for another half an hour – Karen and Jackie both searched on the right hand side of the creek, whilst I made my way down the actual creek to make sure I can check both sides. I just felt he was close – I seriously can't even explain it but I just knew we were close.

As I worked my way down I looked to my left and there was Gomez – he was about 2m to the left of the creek and he was lying down, not being able to move. I screamed as soon as I found him to Jackie and Karen who both came rushing over. Whilst they made their way over I was giving Gomez lots of pats and kisses – it was a massive release of emotion for me and I just couldn't believe that we had found him in such a massive bushland. As soon as Jackie and Karen joined me we assessed the situation. Karen had some cat food and started putting that in front of him to see if he would eat which he did. We then immediately called Sharene to let her know we had found him.

As it was quite deep into the bushland we had to think of the best way to get him out. After deciding it would be to carry him to the road where the industrial area was – Karen had the tools to make a sling/stretcher which we carried Gomez on. I was on the back and Karen and Jackie both swapped between holding the front and finding the best way to get to the bottom. Once we made it to the bottom and handed him over to you and you took him to the vet, we all just couldn't believe what happened. We then started the walk back up to where our cars were, and a kind lady picked us all up in her car on the way up the hill. She took us back to where we then shared our details and went our separate ways.

I just was so happy I was able to give you those moments Gwen, it still doesn't make sense to me this day as to why this all happened to me – as mentioned maybe it was my late family dog Rex guiding me – I just don't know – I just couldn't imagine the feeling of not having closure or last moments with someone you would've cherished for so long.

~

KAREN C

Finding Gomez

The day that I was part of a group of people who found Gomez...

I have to admit I was absolutely more determined and more prepared to search for him in the areas that I thought an old boy may get down to but not have the strength to make his way back up. It was the third day that I had met up at the home of Gwen.

The first day I went with my husband. We managed to chat briefly with Gwen as to where and when she last saw her boy Gomez. While talking to her there was a scrub turkey in the side garden. I asked her if she thought Gomez might have gone after it. She wasn't sure if he would as he had not much exposure to them but had barked a few times off the verandah at them. So my husband and I went over the sloped scrub and followed animal paths that I thought an old boy would take. We criss crossed through the thick lantana and followed a few creek beds down to the bottom of an industrial park. After 3 hours we made it back to the house where the volunteers were all leaving for the day and I agreed I would return the next day.

This day I was by myself and teamed up with another lady and we went against our senses and we searched up the hill from the house.

While we searched we both agreed that we really thought Gomez was down the hill, in the bush, because if he was in someone's yard he would have been heard or seen. So we did a little more searching in the lantana bushes and thicker trees.

The third day I was dressed to combat the dense bushes and wore long sleeves, long pants, leather biking boots, gaters, gloves. I had my backpack with a water bladder, secateurs to cut my way deeper and I thought that if I was going to search where I thought he may be I put a circular sarong that I could use as a sling to carry Gomez out by myself if needed.

I turned up at the beginning of the search and asked if anyone wanted to go deeper with me and follow all of the gullies down methodically. Luckily for me Cayden had also made his mind up to look where others had stopped. We started off chatting about where we thought Gomez was. Sometimes I crawled and cut my way through dense bush so we were not always shoulder to shoulder. I was amazed to see Cayden roll over the thick bushes and tried hard not to be scared of snake encounters. Luckily another person Jackie called out to us if she could join us both as she had been separated from the original group and she felt we were on the right track of going up and down the gullies.

Gwen had been advised by a medium that Gomez was near water and I have to admit it kept us or me going. Despite having traversed terrain that an old dog really should not have been able to get past. On our second last gully we came across a brother and sister who were coming up from the industrial estate following gullies. So we were all happy that the harder areas were really being searched. We then made our way back up the gully and went across to what we thought had to be the last one. Gomez surely could not climb the steep rocky embankment. So we agreed to follow it down like the others. Cayden taking the far left bank, Jackie and I criss crossing through the lantana on the right.

I cannot forget Cayden saying that he thought he could see Gomez. Both Jackie and I scrambled to the left side where in a relatively flat and not rocky area Gomez lay. My mouth still goes dry with the adrenaline at finally finding him. He lifted his head and wiggled his tail. Poor boy I kissed on him so hard. I can't tell you what the others were doing as the adrenaline in my body gave me tunnel vision. I got the bladder of water out of my backpack and fashioned a drinking bowl for him to lap. Seeing him drink we were all so emotional. I had some cat food and chicken in my bag for scent and I put a little down for him but he wasn't that interested. Cayden tried to get Gomez to stand but he was weak in his back legs. We couldn't see anything major wrong- no broken bones - but he had soiled around his tail.

I got my phone out to contact the coordinator and I couldn't text or talk... I eventually pressed my microphone to send a message 'we fucking found him!' By this time we knew we were not going to get Gomez back through the thick bush. I had got my circular sarong out and explained that we could put two long branches through and fashion a stretcher. It's funny but once we put Gomez in it he looked so comfortable. I carried the head end and kept kissing his adorable face. He gave me a few licks. I can't say it was easy but there was no way the adrenaline was going to let me give the two branches up despite Jackie asking if she could help... We three were in a trance of disbelief but a silent determination to return Gomez to Gwen. Eventually we made it through the industrial fence and to a car that had Gwen. I really thought we had got to him in time. I saw such a joy spark in him that I still can't believe that he was so terribly weak. Dogs really are the best at hiding pain. All I know is for that 30 minutes carrying Gomez - I couldn't love him more.

~

JACKIE

Thanks Gwen for asking me to write an account although some of it remains a bit of a blur.

Let me do a recount of my day.

I had been watching the Facebook posts during the week, and having come from a family of Labrador owners and having lost our own Lab/ retriever a couple of years prior I felt an attachment to following the story, however, as a full time worker was unable to assist during the week.

I headed to the gym as I often do on a Saturday morning to return home and scan Facebook. The request for fit people to look came into view and I felt compelled to help.

I came prepared with long trousers and hiking poles, but not sure I was really prepared for the task ahead.

I was sent off with a very talkative lady along the road from the house, however, I kept being drawn over to the bush behind the house. Even though we were told it had been searched, I couldn't move away from the thought that it would be easy to miss a dog due to the terrain and landscape over there.

I was initially searching alone, however, following 2 snake sightings, I bumped into Karen and Cayden, and decided that I should join them for safety.

We walked over together to what appeared to be a waterway. It was steep on the other side, so it was decided that it was unlikely Gomez would have gone further across if he had come this way.

So it was decided we should walk in a line with Cayden in the waterway, myself on Cayden's right on the edge and Karen to my right. We then took this course following the waterway down.

We hadn't gone far when we heard Cayden yell, 'I've found him!!'. Karen and I hurried over with intrepidation of his condition. The sheer relief as he lifted his head. His weakness evident but almost his sheer relief to see people.

Karen, the amazing carrier of all things needed was able to pull out some water as I made the phone call to Gwen to let her know the amazing news.

The decision was made to keep heading down the hill. Gomez placed on the sarong with hiking poles used to carry.

Gomez alert but weak during the walk but I think just happy to be with humans. Karen and Cayden carried as I found a track through the bush in front as we worked out by phone with Gwen and Sharene where we could get out. Thank goodness the business was open and Gomez could be returned to his mum.

Certainly handed over with concerns about his weaknesses but with hope that there was a chance.

Devastating then to hear the news that followed, but thankful to have played a small part in returning Gomez to his mum.

Reflective too about my loss of my lab/retriever 3 years prior when I was on holiday, and not having had that opportunity to have been there to say goodbye.

Poem

BY DAN GEMEINHART

Dogs die.
But dogs live, too.
Right up until they die, they live.
They live brave, beautiful lives.
They protect their families.
And love us.
And make our lives a little brighter.
And they don't waste time being afraid of
tomorrow.

RIP Gomez

After everyone left, I went inside and wrote my RIP Gomez post on his page. I suspected that the grief reaction to Gomez's death was going to be enormous, just from talking to the people who were at the house when we returned. My gratitude to the huge number who had grown to love Gomez, needed to include my support in their grief.

This is my post:

RIP GOMEZ

Gomez stayed alive to be found and back with those that love him.

The willpower and strength.

But we needed to listen to the emergency vet, and save him from further suffering.

His heart was failing, he had no sensation in his legs, he had maggots through him, his blood sugar was so low.

He had been through enough and would have been in ongoing pain if not helped to die. Even if they could have helped him to survive this, it would only have been for such a short time as his heart was damaged.

They didn't even know if he had snakebite or ticks contributing to his condition.

I know you all wanted him to survive, and he DID, to be with me, my son and granddaughter caressing him and giving him chicken as he died.

We are having him cremated and will plant a beautiful GOMEZ TREE at Golden Beach when we move to our new home there at the end of November.

I would love it if you could all come there for a REMEMBERING GOMEZ BBQ to celebrate his life and the love you all put into finding him.

I will post the celebration on here.

Now we are all grieving, but we have closure. He did not die alone.

So much love to you all and thanks from the bottom of my heart that I could be with him.

Sharene also posted on our page:

Sharene .... is feeling emotional.

RIP GOMEZ

On Gwen's behalf we just wanted you to know she is no state to respond to your beautiful thoughts at this stage so please don't be offended, but I know you all understand. I believe there was a reason everyone didn't give up after couple of days. This is the 6th Day and Gomez knew he would see his Mum again. Julie and I will definitely go through posts and answer as many questions you have. Please continue to check this site as we will be arranging catch up for all the searchers. You are an amazing group of people. There is lots of doggo love out there.

Julie also posted:

Fly high beautiful Gomez

What a fighter you were.

So many people prayed for your safe return, so grateful you waited for us. Gwen we are all sending you the biggest hug and thinking of you today. Thank you so much again to everyone that helped in some way.

Community Responses
TO RIP GOMEZ POST

My RIP GOMEZ post had 1.500 reactions and 483 comments just on the Searching for Gomez page. The total number of reactions and comments on the Searching for Gomez page and other Facebook pages were 3,488 reactions, 704 comments and 40 shares. Sharene and Julie's RIP posts also had an enormous response.

This was an extraordinary and unprecedented response to a lost dog on the Sunshine Coast, and is evidence of the widespread concern and love which developed for Gomez over only six days.

Here are some of the beautiful comments and tributes:

> Gomee would have gone to heaven a very happy man. He loved you forever and of course he would have been frightened when he was lost. But when he was found all that was forgotten because Mummy was back next to him and stroking him and giving him kisses and telling him how brave he had been and how much you had missed him and loved him even more than

what you did the last time you saw him. He would have glowed on the inside knowing he was safe and loved and treasured.

My heart is breaking for you but so glad you were able to find him and be with him when he crossed over the rainbow bridge. You never gave up, like so any others would have. I admire you for your courage and strength, and I hope to be able to give you a hug one day. Gomez was so lucky to have a beautiful kind hearted soul like you. Sending you so much love and strength. Run free over the rainbow bridge beautiful boy. You will forever be in so many of our hearts.

You know, I think of you every day., and I'm crying writing this ..but I am so so glad you got to find and see your boy before he crossed over.. I was there the day you found him. I drove past your home and the girls yelled out 'he's been found' .. and I couldn't believe it - I screamed .: I was so happy.. but I'm still sad he's gone - as are you! I just want you to know that you touched sooooo many people with your dedication and love for that beautiful boy! RIP Gomez.

I couldn't sleep that week with worry for Gomez and for you. That horrible sick feeling when your dog goes missing and all the scenarios that your mind plays out. My heart leapt when I read he was found and broke for you all when you had to let him go. I shall never forget his little face or your strength and hope while he was missing. Someone wrote a comment that they carry a little bit of Gomez in their heart - I think we all do. He was a special boy to bring so many together.

He brought a community together, we were all hoping with all of our hearts he would be found. I am sad he has crossed the rainbow bridge but comforted that he knew he was loved by you.

I'm so sorry for your loss. Such a brave, strong boy. Gwen you are so strong.

Sending you much love, it is so hard when our doggies pass, I still think what could I have done better for my Lucy. Then I remember how much I loved her & she knew I did. Gomez would have known that you would move heaven & earth to find him as you did, you got the help you needed and he was there waiting for you, he knew you would always be there for him. Sending love & hugs, please be kind to yourself, xx

I'm so glad he got to see your face once last time. And that after his big adventure he hung on so so long waiting for you to find him.

Poor poor boy. Much love to every human that opened their arms and hearts for this darling boy and his beautiful family. Run free sweetheart.

This has honestly touched my heart as well as so many others. It's never easy losing a loving pet as they are family and become so loved and cared for, but please know that he knows how much he was loved and that's all he needed to know before he couldn't hold on any longer. I am beyond happy he was found and held on that little longer to say his last goodbyes and to see his family one last time before he spread his beautiful wings. Everyone should be so proud of themselves for the amount of effort they put into finding Gomez. Without everyone he may not have been found. Although the outcome is quite sad, the family now have the closure they deserve and he didn't die alone. I am so so sorry for your loss and know that we all have you in our thoughts. Hold your pups a little tighter tonight.

He knew you were coming for him. He held on for as long as he could so he could be with you for his last moments. So heart-breaking.

Oh Gwen, we are so sorry for your loss. So glad, though, that Gomez got to spend his final moments surrounded by your love. What a beautiful dog! We all loved him without even knowing him. So glad he got to live his best life with you. He was truly loved! Thinking of you and sending our love.

I'm so sorry and sad to read this. My heart goes out to you during this difficult and sad time. He held out till you were reunited again and you both got to say goodbye to each other... and that is pure love.

RIP beautiful Gomez. You are loved by so many and brought everyone together. Such a brave boy to wait long enough to be with your family.

Your love and resilience in finding your beautiful boy is nothing short of amazing. I'm sure he will be looking over you.

To love is to let them go... I'm so happy that he could pass with his family Gwen. You never gave up and neither did any of the searchers. He's at peace and was loved so very deeply which is what we as guardians try to do. Much love to you.

You had a plan Gwen, for his end. It didn't go as you thought, but in the end, you got to hold him, you got to tell him how much he was loved, and when he got his wings and soared above you, you were the one he saw holding him. Much love.

The final gift we give our beloved pets is the hardest gift of all. You have done the right thing – he found you again and the memories of that last week would have been lost to him as you held him tight for that last time. RIP precious boy.

This is a beautiful but very sad story of a community bringing Gomez home to spend final hours with his loved ones.

My heart is broken. I'm so sorry Gwen. Gomez has touched so many hearts, particularly this week. I'm so glad you got to hold him before he grew his angel wings. RIP beautiful boy. As a former goldie owner for 15 years also, I know how special these beautiful dogs are. Fly high Gomez.

RIP Gomez. I didn't know you but you sounded like such a beautiful boy. I don't know why I'm crying so much, probably because I'm so sad for you his family, but also happy you got to find him and comfort him as he died. I am in awe of this amazing community that got together and managed to find him. Absolutely amazing.

Thinking of you all and your dear precious Gomez. Our lives are richer for having been involved in the search and seeing such an incredible display of human kindness.

So sorry for your loss. He certainly was a fighter and I am so glad you are least got to say goodbye. Gomez has touched so many here on the coast now.

I'm so sorry to hear about your loss. You've been incredible the last few days and I hope if I ever have to face such a challenging situation I can face it with the strength and determination that you have. I hope you can find comfort in the amount of people sharing your grief after hearing about this heartbreaking situation. I can safely say myself and most likely hundreds of other people who have heard about this story are shedding a tear after hearing this news. I am grateful to know you were reunited albeit for such a short time, and that you were able to comfort him through his last moments in this life. I wish you all the best for the future and hope that our paths cross again, albeit in happier circumstances. RIP Gomez.

It's the final moments that count. He died with his love, and free from his frail body and physical form. His soul will always live on and be in your every heartbeat. Sending you all so much strength and love.

RIP you darling boy. What a story you could have told. My heart is breaking for you and those whose paths you crossed. Play happily over the rainbow bridge.

It is so typical of Gomez to find the strength to make it back home to pass with his loved ones saying goodbye. Gomez the Braveheart.

So so sorry to hear this, but so happy that you got to say good-bye. Run free Gomez. There are hundreds of people who did not know you, but loved you just the same.

I'm so sorry for your loss. Such a heartbreaking time for you but what a beautiful bitter-sweet reunion. Forever in all our hearts.

So so tragic beloved Gomez has passed, but wonderful he held on and was found and able to be with his loving family in his final moments. My heart breaks for all who loved him...and they are many.

To his dear family...you can grieve knowing you and all the wonderful volunteers on the ground at Buderim gave your all to do him well. I'm sorry for your loss.

You will be so missed by us all
May you run around in heaven with a ball,
In the end you were surrounded by love,
I know you'll be barking down from above,
We searched high and low for you boy,
I hope you're up there playing
with your favourite toy.
When we heard the news we shed tears,
You were so adored over all of these years,
Between us all we helped bring you back,

We worked together tirelessly as a pack,
Your beautiful mum adored you so much,
I'm so glad she held you with her loving touch,
One last pat, chicken and cuddles,
Gorgeous Gomez enjoy those heavenly puddles,
You've touched this community far and wide
Sunny coast I have so much pride,
Gomez, such a strong and brave boy
Fly high, you brought so much joy.

He was in the arms of love when he passed and that's all that matters. His memories of that will carry him high. Rest now Gomez, soar high with your beautiful angel wings.

I'm so saddened to read this news, but truly thankful Gomez was able to be with his family and not out in the bush alone suffering any longer. I'm also deeply humbled to witness such an enormous community spirit in the search for him today, to see all these strangers come together was amazing.

What a tough boy Gomez was to endure all of that. He obviously was waiting for you.

Love and prayers for Gomez, yourself, your family and Priya. So very grateful he was found to be with you for that time. He was a trooper to the very end.

I am sorry we couldn't find him sooner for you. He was so beautiful and was obviously waiting for you. Gomez had a wonderful life and was so loved. We are all grateful for that. RIP beautiful boy, my heart goes out to you at this sad sad time.

I am so glad you got reunited with your baby after what probably felt like a lifetime of waiting to find him. However, my heart is absolutely breaking for you...he would have known just how loved he was in those last moments together. How humbling it is to know that the community came together so beautifully to help look for your fur baby. It restores my faith in humanity somewhat to know that beautiful people still exist. Despite how difficult the last few days have been for you, I have no doubt that you have an endless bank of precious memories with Gomez.

There is something to be said that he held on long enough to be reunited with his people, and that speaks volumes of the true nature of a dog. RIP Gomez.

He was so lucky to have you.

I'm so glad he was found and that you got to spend some time with him before he passed. My heart broke for you that day.

> So very sad. So very sorry. Blessed you were with him as he crossed over. He needed you the most then. He had a loved life. Thanks to those who found him.

> I think of Gomez's final steps...he never made it to the road, or the very top of the driveway, he would have been seen. His last poop on the driveway was him turning to take flight into the bushland after that turkey...his only option was to go with the topography to the lowest point. That's my 'if only', 'what if'...pathetic of me to run that over and over in my head...the clues were there for us. Emotions...that is what gets in the way. I'm truly sorry for your loss Gwen.

Apart from these very beautiful comments, which are testament to the love felt for me and for Gomez, I received beautiful gifts from a large number of people. Beautiful cards and flowers started arriving that evening. Gifts over the next few months included drawings of Gomez and one of Gomez and Priya, a shadow box, a leadlight keepsake of the seaside, framed pictures of Gomez and a photo album. Narelle called around a few evenings after Gomez died with the most beautiful video she had made of Gomez's life from my posts about him on his page. Somebody else sent me a cushion cover with his picture on it. I was offered a pure bred Golden Retriever pup, but I did not feel that I could accept it. I was also offered a kitten, but once again I could not accept. Others realised how difficult Gomez's death was for my granddaughter, and she was given a toy Golden Retriever puppy, a lifelike hand made baby doll, framed pictures and a photo album of her with

Gomez. A book was recommended which I purchased, called "The Invisible Leash".

As time went on, people also inquired about Priya, and we went on playdates with other dogs. Priya struggled for some time, and was obviously quite confused. Gomez was not there anymore, and she had always been used to being with another dog. I was grieving, so she would have felt my emotion. As an anxious dog, she finds it hard when I am sad or distressed. Her most noticeable grief reaction was when we moved to Golden Beach and I unpacked furniture and a rug that had been in storage since we left Melbourne. She sniffed it and whimpered as she rolled on the rug and pushed herself against the sofa. So sad.

> The love we get from our pups is so pure and unconditional, it makes us better people…' be the person your dog thinks you are'…and the loss of that is so painful. Learning to accept that love, and then live with the loss are big lessons indeed
>
> ~ Dean Koontz

Finding Gomez

AN ACCOUNT WRITTEN BY KYLIE

The doggo we never met but loved with all our hearts.

Where do I start.......I suppose with how I felt coming into this search situation and what I can only imagine was one of the most stressful times in life for Gwen and her family. As much as I felt for all the humans involved it was Gomez that my heart truly ached for.

I came into the situation at a personally vulnerable time. I had recently experienced the loss of my beautiful Labrador Jack on September 30th. He was my soul mate...heart dog...best friend....all the things. I loved him so much. He was an old man when he passed, his mobility was shot, he was riddled with arthritis and to be fair, I had probably held onto him for longer than was fair for him.

I added all the medications as he aged to help him.....the anti-inflammatories, the joint support, the analgesic tablets and injections. I had mats running all through the house to help him get around and I got rid of my bed and we all slept on the mattress on the floor.

It was only when we had a visit from Dr Sarah and she said 'Oh mate.....he's in so much pain'...that I could see things as they truly were. After 2 weeks of being spoilt rotten and eye fillets every day we gave my beautiful Jack a very dignified and gentle passing at home. He looked so peaceful and it was so heart breaking and perfect.

So I was still very much in a state of grief when I heard about Gomez going missing.

I saw the post, I saw his beautiful face and thought oh no.....this is not OK for an old boy. He needs to be found. I need to help.

My memory is a little sketchy about timelines, when I went, how often I went etc.

My Brother, Dave was there from the beginning to the end and to be fair I feel like I was just along for the ride with him. Safety in numbers and all that....though the actual truth is that the bushland where we thought Gomez may be in was quite scary. I'm not one to go for a bushwalk or be out in nature at the best of times and I'm not super keen on sharing personal space with snakes and spiders so this was not my comfort zone.

But it is Dave's comfort zone. His love of nature, comfort in the bush and love for all creatures shines through in his actions and every day life. Gomez got him from the beginning. He was searching as soon as he knew that Gwen needed help to find her boy. He was on foot in that dense bushland every day, mapping it as he went and he had his drone out in the early hours to try to locate Gomez with thermal imaging.

Before I went searching I asked Dave if he thinks I should help too and he said yes.....Gwen will appreciate all the help she can get.

I think Dave searched every day....sometimes alone, sometimes with his work colleague and sometimes with me. I'm sure I slowed him down but figured we also had 2 sets of eyes scanning the dense bush-

land. He is so humble about his involvement and committed so much time and energy.

He so badly wanted Gomez to be found.

I remember the very first time I went to search..... I spoke to a neighbour who was more than happy that I access his land and search around for Gomez.....we spoke about how Gomez may have chased a bush turkey down the steep bushy embankment at the back of his property.....I wish I had just jumped straight in at this spot and headed down.....follow the trajectory of what was most likely the path Gomez had taken.....bugger the snakes and spiders!

Written from the perspective of searching in the bush......

The bushland was dense, steep, slippery and dangerous. I was equipped with a torniquet, snake bandages, water, shmakos and basically no clue. I feel like I added stuff with each search as I learnt how unforgiving and bitey the bushland can be.....you definitely need proper grippy boots, long pants, long sleeved shirt, gloves, eye protection and even a machete or something to whack the bush away with. There are so many plants and weeds that are out to trip you up, strangle you or bury their thorny little spikes deep into your skin at every opportunity.

Bushland is pretty from a distance......I don't find it pretty up close.

I searched one day with a work mate and we went more around the peripheries and driveways and the easier to access bushland. Once I teamed up with my Bro the search got real. We were most definitely in the thick of it. But with my Bro with me I am so much braver. We carried iphones to map our tracks so we could share these within the group so different areas could be covered by the other searchers. The free app is called GPS tracks.

Dave is an Environmental Scientist and owns his own business. He works so hard, has the best work ethic of anyone I know and although he is so time poor he committed to finding Gomez. He is so unassuming, and he loves dogs with all his heart. During the time I spent in the bush with him he took it upon himself to teach me the names of plants.... scientific name, genus and species. It's a whole different language. He would test me later and I would fail 100% of the time. I just saw them all as plants that were trying to harm me in a landscape that was not fit for a beautiful old golden boy.

The longer we were in that bushland the less hopeful I felt about finding Gomez as time was ticking.

Each morning I would check the Facebook site.....nope....this boy is still out there. I remember one night as I got into bed it was raining and I felt horrible about Gomez being out in it. I wondered how Gwen could get any moments to sleep with this stress. This just seemed so unfair. I later found out from Gwen that she basically didn't sleep and felt like an absolute mess.

Dave led the charge with search areas to cover and where he wanted to look.....and I tagged along.

On the final day of searching we had pushed over to an area that ran down behind the neighboring property and we lapped up and down a few times. As we made our final ascent we heard voices and then someone fell over.... I called out 'are you ok?' It was Karen....there was a brief chat from a distance about the area we had just covered and we continued on.

Karen and the searchers she was with found him soon after........this was a moment of pure joy.....I will discuss this later.

~

Where did we think Gomez had gone?

It's only in hindsight that it seems the most likely thing is that Gomez chased a brush turkey down a steep embankment and just kept moving further down the slope and further and further away from his home.

At the time I had many thoughts about what may have happened and my Bro and I discussed some of these while searching.

He could have gone in any direction! He could be in a backyard, he could be in somebody's house, someone may have taken him.....we simply didn't know.

But the most obvious place was the bush. And there was a lot of it!

What were my feelings about Gomez and how did they change?

I felt like I knew Gomez. I'm sure this is because of the journey I had just been through with Jack. I guess I somewhat morphed them into the same dog for that period of time.

They both had old man faces, were similar colours and body types, both had arthritis and mobility issues, both were dependent on their medications and they both were magical creatures that depended on their humans who loved them with all their heart.

I imagined Jack laying in the bush waiting to be found as he couldn't walk.

The more time that passed the more I couldn't stop thinking about Gomez.

My Bro would text me and say he still hasn't been found and he's heading out again.

We were committed and loved an old boy who we had never met.

Dave also has 2 senior dogs. He is a true dog whisperer and all my dogs have always loved him more than they love me ....except Jack....haha!

Why we turned up day after day

We turned up day after day because Gwen kept asking for help and accepting help and we were simply invested in the finding the sweet old man who had now captured the heart of a community. The old soul with the tear stained face who had now been missing for way too long and hadn't had his medications. I know how important this is and it hurt my heart to imagine how his poor old body was feeling without his meds...wherever he was.

This is probably one of the worst experiences I could imagine going through as a dog owner. And you showed up Gwen day after day....you were open to everyone and everything and accepted it all. You were so vulnerable yet so strong as you reached out to a group of strangers for help....allowing them into your world at a very stressful time. This showed how much you loved Gomez.....you didn't give up....ever.

Dave was never going to give up the search.

What it was like for us when he was found.

I will never forget the moment when we learnt that Gomez had been found.

Oh my god.

Dave and I were walking out of the bushland to the front yard where a group was gathered. Someone yelled out to us that he had been found....and yes...he's alive. This was THE best moment. Goose bumps for days, tears of joy and pure happiness.

I hugged Priya, Gwen's other golden retriever, who was sitting with a woman (as Gwen was mobile in a car to meet up with Gomez and his rescuers) and told her that her Brother had been found. She was probably wondering why this stranger was crying and laughing and being such a weirdo.

The next searchers came in from the bush and we yelled out to them "He's been found"! Everyone was just so bloody happy and the mood was high.

The next question was how his health was and will he be OK.

So off we went to celebrate......back home to hug our doggos. Dave suggested a pie party to celebrate as this is a family tradition for Doggo birthday celebrations.

Bro got the Beefy's pies, I went home via the main street of Buderim and took down all the lost dog posters I had plastered to bins and poles and shops, and everything felt great. I told anyone who asked that he had been found!

All the doggos gathered at my place and Mum joined us to celebrate as she had been following the journey with us. We ate our pies and talked about Gomez and the search and how amazing it was that he had been found.

Then we read the update that Gomez had been put to sleep. He was not in great shape and Gwen had made the most difficult decision to let him go. I cried. We probably all did.

But in my heart I still felt a sense of relief that Gomez had been found, was back with his person and was no longer suffering. This is huge.

~

The whole experience and what it meant for me.

So, in a nutshell, I've never been involved in searching for a lost dog before. Gomez just had a face that made us want to find him....and a human who wasn't giving up on him even when things seemed very dire.

I learnt a lot....about human nature, about the community we live in and about searching bushland for a lost dog. Lessons were learned for next time.

It hurt my heart a lot and I know that I was still grieving my old boy at the time too.

I thought I can't get involved in anything like this ever again......yet here we are. Gomez left a legacy and it's an honour to be a part of it.

So much love for a doggo we never met.

I feel like Jack was a big part of my personal journey during the time we searched for Gomez. Hope the old boys are running around together in doggo heaven eating pies.

Gomez and Charlotte

From the first time that Gomez and Priya met my granddaughter Charlotte, they were fascinated by this little human and the noises she made. Priya would lie down on the ground so as to appear non threatening, as she had always done when she was close to a child. It was clear that Priya could tell that this new little human was important to us all, and Priya knew that she had to look after her. Gomez seemed happy to have Charlotte around, but was not as entranced as Priya.

Gomez was already a senior dog when Charlotte was born, so although he seemed happy about her, I was not entirely sure that he might not growl or snap at her if she hurt him unintentionally. From when she was quite young, Charlotte spent two days a week with me, and I always made sure that any interactions between her and the dogs were supervised. I did not think that I could trust Gomez fully, and have also always been aware of the need for that supervision.

If Gomez and Priya had any doubts about this little person, these were quickly dissipated when Charlotte started to have solid food. She became a wonderful food source. At first they found that if they sat close to me when she was being fed, some food would always drop down to their level. As she grew bigger, and sat in a high chair and then had her own little table and chair, they could see the great benefit of staying close and waiting patiently for the wondrous food that they could gather.

When Charlotte arrived at my house in the morning, she would greet the dogs before me. She came with me to the dog park on the days that she spent with me. It was clear that Charlotte was growing up to become a true dog person. She got to know the names of all the regular dogs at the dog park, and loved watching them all play and fetch the ball. She learnt from an early age to be sensible around dogs and never to approach a dog without checking with me first.

Charlotte was always loving and gentle with the dogs, and really enjoyed her interactions with both Priya and Gomez. She liked putting hats and other clothing items on them, enjoyed throwing toys for them, and talked to them gently and sweetly. Like me, she enjoyed her "conversations" with them. Charlotte mastered the basic command words, and also learnt that "D-I-N-N-E-R" spelled dinner. She loved them with all her heart.

Charlotte used to lie on Priya (and still does) when she wanted to relax with a book or a game on her phone, and also to watch television. I did not let her lie with her full weight on Gomez because I thought it might hurt him. Charlotte found other ways to be very close to Gomez. She started to realise that Gomez needed extra special care because he was old. I would explain his problems to her, and her heartfelt and empathic responses were so beautiful. She loved him so much and recognised his vulnerability. She knew that he needed extra time when we were walking the dogs, or when we were getting them into the back of the car, and developed patience in her interactions with him. She understood that he could no longer hear properly and so needed clapping or a high pitched voice to know what was happening. Charlotte also understood that he was in pain at times and hated it if he bumped into something, or struggled to get up onto the kerb. She learnt so much from spending a lot of time with an older vulnerable dog. Charlotte was so affectionate with him and was always hugging him and patting him.

When Gomez went missing, we were all living in the same house, so Charlotte knew about it straight away. We told her that a lot of people were helping us to try to find him, and that we hoped that he would be back home soon. For the first few days she asked me when he would come home, and checked if he was back first thing in the morning. As the days went on, it was obvious that Charlotte's little heart was breaking as she lost hope, and she stopped asking me when he would come home.

The day that Gomez was found and taken to the Emergency Vet, my son and Charlotte met me there. I was so pleased that Charlotte's parents knew the importance of her saying a proper goodbye to Gomez. When they arrived, my son was paying the vet bill and Charlotte and I talked. I was feeling so many different emotions, but I think I was able to talk to Charlotte in the way that she needed. Having been through it before with my other much loved senior dogs, I described for her what was about to happen.

This was Charlotte's first experience of the death of a being that she was close to. And she was about to turn five years of age the next day. So young to understand what was happening and to be able to process the rush of different emotions she would be feeling. Like the rest of us, she was no doubt relieved that he had been found at last. But, like the rest of us, she did not want to have to say goodbye so soon.

We went in to see Gomez, and Charlotte loved the purple velvet they had put over him. Her favourite colour. Gomez looked so peaceful and there was no sign of the damaged body that I had witnessed ten minutes before. He looked like he was already having a wonderful nap with a purple velvet blanket to keep him warm. The vet described what would happen and brought out the chicken. This was wonderful for Charlotte as it gave her, and my son and I, something to do at such a very sad time. We stroked his head and told him we loved him. Even though Gomez was sedated he gobbled down the chicken, until he died, and his mouth stopped moving.

We were all crying. It was just such a very sad ending to such a very difficult week. It was not the outcome that any of us wanted, but I know that Charlotte, my son and I all felt that Gomez knew we were there with him, when it counted. I know that I hoped that the horrible week that he had endured melted away with our presence and touch. We hugged each other as we left the room.

I had told Charlotte that we would find a star which would show us where Gomez had gone in the sky. I had also said that we would plant a Gomez tree to remember him by. The first night, Charlotte and I went outside and I asked her which star she thought was Gomez looking down on us. She chose the bright one closest to the moon, because in her words: 'We loved him to the moon and back'.

Over the next week or so, it was clear that Charlotte was having difficulty processing her grief. I decided that she needed a photo album of Gomez, and Suzanne put that together for me. Charlotte and I also have identical framed photos of her with Gomez, mine in my living room and Charlotte's in her bedroom. Kellie gave her a photo frame and a sweet necklace with a dog on it. For Christmas, Kellie gave Charlotte a beautiful hand made lifelike baby doll. A few weeks after Gomez died, Helen gave Charlotte a life size Golden Retriever stuffed toy, which she still loves. I read her a book about losing a much loved dog. Charlotte also helped me to choose the hibiscus which we later planted at Golden Beach.

Like an adult, for a child the grief of losing a much loved dog does not get processed easily or quickly. In the days following Gomez's death, I noticed that Charlotte was not the same with Priya, and seemed to be avoiding close contact with her. No doubt she now realised that loving a dog could also lead to the pain of losing a dog. That did not last long, and their resumed close relationship was a comfort to them both. Charlotte and I often talk about Gomez and look at photos of him together. We laugh about the funny things he did, and are sad about his aging, going missing and his death. It is a bond that Charlotte and I share, and our memories of him have only strengthened our relationship further.

I know that both Charlotte and I feel so lucky to have loved and been loved by our precious boy Gomee.

Grief

Grief, I've learned
is really just love.
It's all the love you want to give
but cannot. All that unspent love gathers up
in the corners of your eyes,
the lump in your throat,
and in that hollow part of your chest.
Grief is just love with no place to go.
~ Jamie Anderson

Like everyone who reaches a certain age, I have had a lot of experience with grief. My mother had unresolved grief from the loss of her first child, not through death, but through severe disability and the family decision to institutionalise him, which in effect, hid him away. She never forgave herself and had no healthy outlets for her grief and guilt. She parented the rest of her children, with me as the youngest, under the shadow of this grief and this guilty family secret. I remember asking her who was with her in a photo which was on a sideboard. She burst into tears and my father reprimanded me, saying I was never to ask that question and upset my mother like that. So I grew up knowing about grief before I could name it.

Then there were my own losses and the associated grief. The deaths of my grandparents, my family dog, my mother, my favourite aunt, my father and other dogs. My divorce, the end of significant relationships and friends, moving from one area to another, changing jobs, retiring, losing friends and losing good health are all losses which have impacted me.

As a Social Worker, a large part of my work related to grief and loss, particularly as I moved into the specialised area of adoption. The losses in this area of work were massive, for the child, for the birth parents (who had lost their child due to family circumstances, cultural expectations or poverty), and for the adoptive parents who had normally experienced infertility, recurrent miscarriages or stillbirth. I worked in this area, amidst the grief, for more than thirty years. During this time, I also taught Community Welfare at TAFE, and one of the electives was Grief and Loss. At Ultimo TAFE I became the person who specialised in this elective, and I taught it for some years. One could say that I gradually became an 'expert' in grief and loss, knowing all the current theoretical approaches, understanding the day-to-day experience of grief, and, as a highly empathic person, feeling the experiences of others.

I am grateful for my understanding of grief, as it has helped me to appreciate that there is no "right" or "wrong" way to handle loss. Labels of "pathological grief" are not as often applied professionally nowadays, but our culture does judge others for how they grieve. If a woman sets a place at the table for her late husband who has just died, that may be acceptable, but if he died ten years ago, is that seen as inappropriate by her family and friends? Is it really inappropriate, if she is still able to gradually learn to function and move forward in her life? Or is it just that it makes others feel uncomfortable?

When we grieve we are not just feeling sad. We experience a wide range of emotions. Some grief theorists have become known for arranging these in a sequence, or in stages, with the expectation that at the end, we accept our loss. Knowing what to expect can be helpful for some, but often these theories are limiting. They can make grief into something which is prescriptive and neat, tidying up the messy emotions which recur and recur for many years after a significant loss. Our culture does not like messy emotions, and we have very few effective rituals to support those experiencing grief. Bereaved people have described others crossing to the other side of the road to avoid them. The truth is that those people crossing to the other side of the road are generally not heartless, but probably just do not know what to say. If something is said, it is so often trite and formulaic, often referring to 'time healing'. It is never that simple.

I have always been interested in the way that different cultures approach loss and grief. Most have very different belief systems, and accepted rituals to deal with grief. I have been lucky enough to have known my Balinese 'brother', who is a spiritual leader in his village, for over thirty years. Over those years, I have been privileged to be included in Balinese Hindu rituals and ceremonies. The great certainty of what has to be done in order to protect the spirit of the deceased, and the belief in reincarnation are never questioned. That faith is something that I have never experienced myself. When my father died, I spent time in Bali, which helped me to process my feelings and to see his loss quite differently, as I participated in the cleansing ceremonies and cremation of a Balinese woman I had known for some years. This experience, compared to my father's cremation in Australia, was consoling and freeing. I am so grateful for the inclusion in another culture that I have been given by my relationship with my Balinese brother, Dewa.

The intensity of grief experienced when we have a significant loss seems to be directly related to the intensity of the love we shared with that person or animal. How much we needed them in our lives, how they perceived us, how they made us feel and how we feel without them. Our grief can be complicated by many things. Unresolved issues make our grief complicated. Guilt makes our grief complicated. Not being understood makes our grief complicated. Feeling responsible in some way makes our grief complicated. The expectations of others to 'move on' or 'get over it' makes our grief complicated. Not being able to express our grief in a safe environment makes our grief complicated. I have also discovered that grieving "in the public eye" makes our grief complicated.

What I have learned from my personal and professional experience of grieving, is that when we are grieving, we need to do what we need to do. As our culture does not have clear rituals, apart from a funeral, perhaps a wake and sometimes memorials, we have to find what works for us. Just about anything is okay, if it helps us to slowly work through our emotions. Pushing our emotions down, putting them aside "until later", or numbing them through substances, does not help, as we are going to feel the emotions at some stage. There is no short cut, and the passing of time, seen as the panacea for grief, can take away some of the emotional intensity, but does not fully heal grief. Grief is just tough and painful. Our challenge is to find a way to integrate our emotions and memories, so we can still function in the world. We also need to find a way to express the love we felt for that person or animal. At first it can feel like our challenge is to just breathe.

The grief of losing a dog is one that is hard to understand for those who have not had a loving relationship with a dog. Many have no idea how losing a dog can break our heart. When Monty died, I told my employer that I could not take any work on for a few weeks, as a family member had died. I knew that if I said my dog had died, I would not have had such a compassionate response, unless the person I told was a true dog lover.

The unconditional love, dependence and trust that a dog has for their human is unique, and is the reason that dogs have become companion animals over time. Not only can they protect our physical selves from harm, but they can guard and nurture our emotional life. Dogs forgive, they live for the moment, they wait for us, they rarely complain and they find joy in simple things. They teach us lessons which we need to learn. If we are happy and excited, our dog mirrors those emotions, even when they do not understand the reason for our feelings. They are happy and excited simply because the person they love is feeling that way. A dog looks into your eyes and sees a perfect human, with no judgement about appearance, achievements or status. A loving dog sees us as wonderful and helps us to see ourselves in a more positive light. They do not say to us 'get over it', 'don't worry about it' or 'don't be silly'. Instead they are just there, lovingly present. If we can see ourselves through the eyes of our loving dog, we can see ourselves at our best. Losing a dog means losing that non judgemental source of love.

Losing a dog is incredibly painful, and the grief is often compounded by guilt. The guilt may come from wondering if we let them live too long, or if we cut their lives short, or if we gave them enough when they were with us, to if we are responsible in some way. Dogs are totally dependent on their human, so that leads to guilt. Most people who have lost a dog have questions they ask themselves which intensify their grief and guilt. I will always regret that Gomez was alone for those 5 days, as I know how scared he would have been. It has been so hard feeling like I failed him when he needed me most, and apart from mourning him, that guilt has been so difficult to get through.

The guilt that I felt when Gomez went missing is shared by many dog parents. The recurrent thought of "if only" can be a very destructive one. In my case, there were so many "if onlys". 'If only I had checked that the garage door fob worked that day', 'if only I had checked the dogs sooner that day', 'if only I had followed Priya's early indicator of where Gomez might have gone', 'if only I had not followed advice that dogs have a favourite way to turn, and told searchers that he likely turned to the left at the top of the drive', 'if only I had decided sooner that he must have gone into the bush'. These thoughts, which still visit me at dark times or in the middle of the night, have made my grief harder to bear. I am such a dog lover, and I have always taken my responsibility as a dog parent very seriously. They are dependent on me to care for them, to cuddle them, to take them out each day, to play with them and to check that they are comfortable and safe. I had a very strong feeling that I had let Gomez down, and that he was on his own, scared, and possibly injured, because I had not kept him safe. I had an image of him in my mind, alone and scared, wondering why I was not there with him to help. I knew the panic he felt if he could not find me for a few minutes, let alone a few days. I still get that image of him alone and scared in my mind, particularly when I wake in the middle of the night. I did not feel judged by others, who saw how much I loved Gomez, and how hard I worked to make sure that he was found, but it was a judgement I made of myself.

In the case of losing a dog, there are certainly no clear rituals, as it is not universally accepted that losing a dog is a significant loss. I have always had my own rituals, such as putting together a photo book or frame and planting a tree. I chose a beautiful hibiscus for Gomee, which I call my "Gomee Tree". With the cream colour and red heart, I knew it was the one for him. It is still small, but it is growing with the love I had for him and the soil which contains his ashes.

Many dog lovers have, over time, developed a set of beliefs which have helped them, and then helped others. There is a widespread belief that dogs grow wings when they die, and go to the Rainbow Bridge. They have no more pain, but run around joyfully with other dogs until the day their human comes to join them. In the meantime, they watch over their human, and give signs that they are nearby, in the forms of butterflies, cloud shapes and the human feeling that they are nearby. There are numerous poems and paintings reflecting these beliefs, and these can be very consoling when grieving a dog. It is like the equivalent of heaven, angels and being watched over that some believe when they lose a precious person in their lives.

When Gomez died, I received hundreds of messages from people who had known about him, or helped to search for him, and most of those messages contained references to these beliefs. I have never been particularly religious, and my view on death was that nothing much happens after death. I have always liked the idea of reincarnation, but it has not been my firm belief or consolation. At times in my life I have wished that I had some beliefs that would help me in my grief. When I lost Gomez, I found that I took on the beliefs described above. I needed something more powerful than my previous beliefs and rituals, and these new beliefs were reassuring and comforting. How could a precious old soul like Gomez just be gone, so suddenly. He would have to make sure I was okay. It started to feel like his last act of love for me was to bring a community together to find him, and then for that community to be there for me when I needed solace and understanding. Most of these people were also grieving Gomez's loss, even though the majority had never met him. It all felt a bit magical, but it helped me feel less alone.

I am so grateful for the Gomez community who have helped me to keep remembering to breathe through the trauma and grief of losing my precious old boy.

Don't Cry Sweet Mama

POEM BY EMMA ROSE LEWIS

Don't cry sweet Mama, please don't weep.
Please try dear Mama, to get some sleep.
I know you're sad, and it's because of me.
But don't cry Mama, for now, I am pain free.

I know you miss me, and I miss you too,
No one could have loved me more than you.
I know of some dogs that run away to die,
But not me Mama, I looked you straight in the eye.

I didn't want to leave you, but my body lost the fight.
And now my dearest Mama, you mourn me day and night.
You wished you could have given me a bit more time to live.
But Mama, believe me, I had little left to give.
I am glad you took me on that day, there was no other choice.
I would have told you to 'do it' - if I had a human voice.
Don't feel guilty Mama, I know it broke your heart.
I was always going to leave you first, we knew it from the start.

But what a life you gave me, it really was the best.

Not many have a life like mine, for that, I am truly blessed.
I hope one day I will see you again,
With a smile upon your face.
But for now, I will snuggle up inside your heart,
My very favorite place.

Remembering Gomez

HIS LEGACY

Gomez's Facebook page has continued on since his death in October 2022, and is a beautiful page full of stories, photographs and funny videos of Gomez, Priya and many other dogs. It is now called "Remembering Gomez". I often put posts up, starting with 'Hello wonderful people'. Sharene and I have made it a private group after a few strange profiles started to find their way onto the page.

The Remembering Gomez page is a way for me to honour Gomez, share memories about him and to remain connected to the wonderful community who found him for me. Remembering Gomez has also become a well known Facebook page for people to put up posts of missing dogs. Sometimes people join the group to put up a post about their missing dog, or sometimes an existing member of the group puts up a missing dog post. It also includes posts on ways to help if a dog goes missing, so that the group who came together to find Gomez can add to their knowledge of what to do if they know of a dog who is missing.

As "admins" on the page *Remembering Gomez*, Sharene and I are very aware that we cannot offer help every time a dog goes missing.

So many dogs go missing on the Sunshine Coast, particularly when there are storms or fireworks. Even when owners think that they have secured their dogs, the extreme panic the dog feels means that they can escape by jumping a fence or sometimes breaking through a flyscreen or gate. Owners who have a dog who is frightened of storms or fireworks can see that the only intention of the dog is just to get somewhere "safe". They go into survival mode due to the terror they experience. Priya is the first dog I have ever had who is terrified of storms and fireworks. I use a "thundercoat" to soothe her, and this works quite well, but these are not effective for all dogs. Apart from running away during storms or fireworks, dogs go missing through gates left open inadvertently, gate and garage door fob malfunction, holes in fences or inadequate fencing. Other dogs may take off when getting let out of the car, or if they are off-lead in a dog park or dog beach and get a fright.

Lost dog pages are full of comments made to help owners work out how to find their dogs, but also inevitably have a number of comments from people judging the owners of dogs who go missing, rather than helping to find the dog. No doubt some owners may be at fault when their dog goes missing, as they have been careless. When this is the case, blaming and judging does no good when owners are already blaming themselves. The dog is missing and scared somewhere, and judging the owner does nothing towards getting that dog safely home. An ongoing problem with social media is the "keyboard warriors" who feel compelled to criticise, judge or blame, not just with lost dogs but with so many posts and pages. We do not tolerate that type of judging on Remembering Gomez, and making the group private has meant that we can have control over that.

In memory of Gomez, Sharene and I focus on dogs who are unlikely to find their own way home, because they are old, deaf, blind, very young, or vulnerable in some way. We have found that most older vulnerable dogs have become used to receiving help in their daily lives, and will not run away from searchers. They are often trapped in a spot, too far down a hill to get back up, or they have been injured and cannot get home. An older dog will become disoriented more easily and even when close to home, may not be able to find their way home again.

Dogs who have been recently rescued and are not bonded to their new home or owners are also particularly vulnerable, but need a particular type of approach, as they are the most likely dogs to quickly revert to their primitive instincts, making them very unlikely to respond to their name or any other prompts in searching for them. We are lucky enough to have some experts in this field, notably Annette Ross, who is very familiar with the way such dogs should be approached when they have gone missing. She has been involved in many successful searches where a dog is vulnerable in that way.

Sharene and I often respond to posts about vulnerable lost dogs by commenting on the post, or messaging the owner privately, when we believe that our group could come together to form a search party, help distribute flyers, doorknock neighbours or search with drones. We will encourage the owner to ask for and accept help, particularly when a couple of days have passed with no success in finding the dog. People are often reluctant to ask for help, and hold back, thinking that they have searched everywhere. I see it as our job to gently encourage them to ask, as in many cases, the more people involved the better. It is easy to miss a dog who is stuck, silent or cannot hear people searching for him/her. So many dogs, including Gomez, would never have been found without the owner asking for help, and the community responding to that.

The people who searched for Gomez, or the "Gomez crew", are still involved in such searches, and are very responsive when somebody asks for help through the Remembering Gomez page. We have had a lot of successes, and each time a dog is found I see it as honouring Gomez and his memory. It is emotional and difficult and sometimes it triggers my memories of the time that Gomez was missing. But the rewards in being part of reuniting loved pets with their families are massive. I find that it is important to me to feel like I am giving back, and honouring those who gave to me so generously when I needed it. Like 'paying it forward'. Some of these dogs have been Lilly, who was a blind senior girl, Ruby, thirteen years old with arthritis, Indie, thirteen years old, deaf and blind in one eye, Bella, who was old, deaf and blind, Bunnie, who was eleven years old, partially blind and deaf, as well as Seamus, Georgia, Charlie and Louis. These dogs were found after a few days, and remained in good health despite their ordeals. A few dogs we heard about sadly did not make it, for example, Reggie, Goldie and another Ruby. Bunnie went missing a second time, and sadly died.

Most people know very little about how to search for their missing dog. I knew nothing, as I had never had a dog go missing before Gomez. Lack of sleep, worry, grief, exhaustion and loss of hope all affect the cognitive abilities of anyone in that situation. Having somebody who has been through the same experience can mean a great deal. Each time a dog is found successfully, we learn a little more about the behaviour of old dogs if they go missing. This gives information and insight which helps in subsequent searches. We have learnt a great deal about what older vulnerable dogs do when they go missing. We learnt a lot with Gomez and now know that he behaved in a typical way for a dog of his age and mobility. Having found his way into the bush, he could not get back up, so went downhill. It is very difficult for an older dog to move uphill as it takes so much effort and strength. It can therefore be anticipated that an older dog will move downhill when there is a slope. The dog may get stuck somewhere, for example in vines and weeds or in a hole, free themselves, then tumble down further as they are exhausted from the physical exertion. We also know that an older vulnerable dog will not go far, and have found most dogs (including Gomez) within 300 metres from home.

While older dogs do not typically go very far, we have learnt that dogs are often able to go further into the bush, where it looks inaccessible, than we would imagine. Many people stop searching deep into the bush, thinking that an old dog could never find their way through. Gomez went further into the bush than most searchers thought he would have. All dogs, including older ones, will try to go to a water source once they smell it.

It is also interesting that most older dogs are different to younger dogs who are lost. Older dogs tend to welcome seeing people, as they know they need help, and perhaps because they have become used to accepting human help as they have aged. The three people who found Gomez all reported that he lifted his head, and even wagged his tail a little, as if to welcome them, knowing that they would help. From their descriptions, I imagine that he was saying to them: 'AT LAST!'

The other way we help with lost dogs is to share their posts on our page, and we have done that with Bowie, Turbo, Jasmine, Luna, Ollie, Axel, Missy, Murphy, Porshia, Tilly, Chopper, Ruby, Toby and Jade, to name a few. We can share the information about how people in the community should behave if they see a dog who is in panic mode, for example, not to call out, not to whistle, not to chase, but instead, to take note of the exact location, and contact the owner or search crew. With each of these delicate rescues, many of which were new placements for rescue dogs, it has been a case of waiting patiently for the dog to be ready to approach. This has often taken many days. As mentioned there are experts in this type of assistance, and their work is amazing. Where we can get the information, we also share updates of how the dogs have been since they were reunited.

It is my hope that we can continue to help in this area, and that lost dogs can be home safely with their families as quickly as possible. We are not experts, but are "learning on the job", and the wonderful feeling when a dog is found is a very special thing. It fills my heart to be able to remember Gomez in this way.

Someone said to me the other day: 'Gomez was honoured by how he lived with you. He was much more than the last chapter.' Some comments mean so much and make such a difference, and that was one of those comments. It is so easy to remember the trauma of him being lost and then losing him. Grief overwhelms me when I focus on his last days. But he was so much more than that.

Gomez lived life to the full and he spent every moment loving, playing and having fun. He faced challenges with courage and loved with all his heart, whether it was me, family, friends, Priya or his ball. There were no half measures for Gomez. He was funny, quirky, adventurous and cheeky. The only time he showed sadness was when his ball was lost. Gomez was so happy and was loved so much. Life revolved around him, Monty and then Priya. Beach holidays, playdates, café time, cuddles, tummy rubs, ball chasing, swimming, running and rumbling. What a life!!

Priya is also part of Gomez's legacy. She loved him and learnt so much from him. She is a precious girl who missed him greatly for some time. I always knew that she would need another dog once Gomez died, as she was so used to doggie company. Priya is much closer to me now, since Gomez died. She enjoys being a single dog as she gets all the attention and affection. The gap she felt when Gomez went has luckily been filled by a new addition to my son's family, an Australian kelpie named Rolo. He has just turned one year of age. Priya and Rolo play together several times a day, and Priya is still managing to keep the upper paw. Together they also enjoy playdates, for example, with Kylie's two dogs.

Gomez was my heart dog, who loved with an enormous heart and was loved by so many. He filled my heart. Gomez will always live in my heart and will never be forgotten. Gomez was courageous, enthusiastic, loving, cheeky, funny and quirky. I know that I have not been the same person since the trauma of him being lost. I was affected by it so deeply, and my heart is still broken. But I also know that I was truly blessed to have him by my side for fifteen years. I am so grateful for the joy, happiness and comfort he brought me in those years, and the unconditional love he gave me so freely. His legacy honours him and the precious love we true dog lovers share with our dogs.

> The opportunity to love a dog and to treat it with kindness is an opportunity for a lost and selfish heart to be redeemed. They are powerless and innocent, and it's how we treat the humblest among us that surely determines the fate of our souls.
>
> ~ Dean Koontz

A Love So Deep

From Kylie:

....he was found because of you and because you loved him so deeply and you didn't give up. I admire you so much for this.

The final chapter for Gomez was not one that you would ever choose.....it was heart breaking. But his legacy is simply amazing. Everyone knows Gomez and even though we never met him we love him. What an amazing loved boy he was.

The Rescuers

TO JACKIE, KAREN C AND CAYDEN

My love and gratitude always to the three of you, who followed your instincts and sensed where Gomez would be. Further into the bush than anybody else imagined he could have ventured.

Everyone involved led to the outcome on the bitter sweet 6th day and the three of you were able to bring closure.

He was waiting for me to make sure that he was found, and you were able to give him the love he needed until he could see me again.

Thank you.

The Rescuers

Acknowledgements

I am grateful to so many for making this book possible.

My family and close friends who have been encouraging and supportive, particularly my son Alex, my sister Philippa, my brother Dave, my nephew Sean, my dear friends Laz, Sharene, Kylie, Jenny, Maxine, Annette, Elizabeth and Zohara.

Members of the Remembering Gomez group who answered my many questions about the time Gomez was missing and why they helped and joined the group. Thanks also to the members of the group who gave me feedback about excerpts of my work, ideas about which photos to use and encouragement to keep going.

Every person who helped to search for Gomez who showed such kindness, generosity, commitment and love. You inspired this book.

Karen C, Cayden, Jackie and Kylie who wrote their accounts as part of the book.

Saskia, who proofread my work and gave me feedback and encouragement. Hayley, who helped enormously with the phase that I found the most challenging – getting the story ready to be published. Simone, who suggested Hayley, and who begs me every time I see her to please finish this book, as she really wants to read it.

The tutors and students in the two U3A writing classes that I have attended. I have learnt a great deal about writing from their input.

My professional knowledge and experience in grief, advocacy and writing.

All the dogs in my life who have loved me unconditionally and given me so much.

My girl Priya who has been so patient when my attention was on writing instead of playing with her.

My heart dog Gomez for the inspiration to write about his life and the love we shared.

Thank you.

About the Author

Gwenda Gray was born in Sydney and lived there most of her life. She was one of four children and grew up on a large bush block.

Gwenda was married in her twenties and has a son, now in his forties. She divorced when he was young and was a single mother. Being a mother has always brought her great joy, and she sees that as her greatest accomplishment in life. She now lives on the Sunshine Coast with her son, daughter-in-law and granddaughter, and her Golden Retriever, Priya.

After six years of boarding school, Gwenda studied to become a Social Worker and worked in that profession for over forty years. She worked in the areas of relationship counselling, youth, drug and alcohol, child protection and mental health. For the last thirty years of her professional life, she specialised in Adoption and worked in Private Practice as an Adoption Assessor. Gwenda also worked as a Counsellor and taught various Community Welfare subjects at Ultimo TAFE.

Gwenda has always had dogs, except for a few years when working full time and a single mother. She grew up with a Labrador and became a dog mum as soon as she could in her early twenties. She has had Golden Retrievers for nearly thirty years.

Gwenda is a natural advocate, whether it is for children, vulnerable adults or animals.

This is Gwenda's first book. She has always enjoyed writing and was experienced in writing detailed assessment reports for her work. She always planned to write once she retired, but with Covid and other distractions, she had not made a start. When her heart dog, Gomez, went missing, a story developed which was unprecedented and bitter-sweet.

It was a story which had to be told.

Remembering Gomez Facebook Group:
Facebook.com/groups/450242990306618

www.ingramcontent.com/pod-product-compliance
Lightning Source LLC
Chambersburg PA
CBHW040224170726
48295CB00014B/805

* 9 7 8 1 7 6 3 6 8 9 6 0 2 *